CAMBRIDGE STUDIES
IN ENGLISH LEGAL HISTORY

Edited by

HAROLD DEXTER HAZELTINE, LITT.D.

Of the Inner Temple, Barrister-at-Law;
Downing Professor of the Laws of England in the
University of Cambridge

INTERPRETATIONS
OF LEGAL HISTORY

T0371581

INTERPRETATIONS
OF LEGAL HISTORY

BY

ROSCOE POUND, Ph.D., LL.D.

Carter Professor of Jurisprudence in Harvard University

CAMBRIDGE

AT THE UNIVERSITY PRESS

1923

CAMBRIDGE UNIVERSITY PRESS
Cambridge, New York, Melbourne, Madrid, Cape Town,
Singapore, São Paulo, Delhi, Mexico City

Cambridge University Press
The Edinburgh Building, Cambridge CB2 8RU, UK

Published in the United States of America by Cambridge University Press, New York

www.cambridge.org
Information on this title: www.cambridge.org/9781107698192

First published 1923
First paperback edition 2013

A catalogue record for this publication is available from the British Library

ISBN 978-1-107-69819-2 Paperback

TO

JOHN HENRY WIGMORE

THE JURIST'S EXPLANATION OF LEGAL DEVELOPMENT IN ENGLAND AND ELSEWHERE

JAMES RUSSELL LOWELL, in one of his letters to Stedman, the poet, remarks: "I think one of the greatest pleasures is to come across a poem that one can honestly like; it's like finding a new flower. If, at the same time," Lowell adds, "one can please the author by telling him so, all the better." These words are as applicable to a piece of juristic writing as they are to a poem. Although they are very different from each other in many ways, both these forms of literature possess at least one marked feature in common. By virtue of its own particular qualities of style and matter, every book on jurisprudential thought, no less than every poem, has the power within itself to give the reader either pleasure or displeasure; it has the faculty of making the reader like it or dislike it. In the present volume of the *Cambridge Studies in English Legal History* the reader comes across a new work on jurisprudence, a history and criticism of certain aspects of juristic thought in England and in other countries; and, whether the reader be lawyer, historian, or philosopher, he will find that this book gives him one of his greatest pleasures, that it calls forth his honest liking, and that, indeed, it is a source of his enlightenment and intellectual stimulus. In Lowell's apt phrasing, the reading of *Interpretations of Legal History* is "like finding a new flower." Such a pleasure comes but rarely to the one who studies the literature of legal history and jurisprudence; and "if, at the same time, one can please the author by telling him so, all the better."

The author of this remarkable book in which, on request, he has embodied his recent Cambridge lectures on the juristic and philosophical explanation of the epochs, processes, and ends of legal development, needs no presentation to the learned reader. The Dean of the Law Faculty and the Carter Professor of

Jurisprudence in Harvard University has long been recognized as one of the foremost jurisprudential thinkers of our time. Dr Pound's oral teaching of the history and principles of Jurisprudence has given learning and inspiration to many of the younger generation of lawyers in our common law jurisdictions; while his writings on jurisprudential subjects have spread his teaching far and wide throughout the world. Many of his essays, covering a wide range of subject-matter, have been published in the legal, philosophical, and historical periodicals of America and Europe. Let us omit all Dr Pound's writings on botany, legal education, and the history and principles of common law and equity: let us name only a few of his scattered papers dealing particularly with juristic thought. Let these few be the following: "Theories of Law," "Legal Rights," "A Theory of Social Interests," "Executive Justice," "Juristic Science and Law," "Law in Books and Law in Action," "The Limits of Effective Legal Action," "Spurious Interpretation," "Mechanical Jurisprudence," "The End of Law as developed in Legal Rules and Doctrines." The learned reader will not need to be reminded that this short list of titles might be greatly extended. Nor will he forget that within recent months three longer writings in the author's chosen fields of research and thought have appeared—the monograph on criminal justice in American municipalities, *The Spirit of the Common Law*, and *An Introduction to the Philosophy of Law*.

In his present volume Dr Pound deals with a vast and complex subject-matter in that lucid and forceful manner familiar to the reader of his other writings and to the listener at his spoken lectures and addresses. His main theme is the juristic and philosophical interpretation of the history and principles of legal systems; and over that theme he throws the spell of his accurate and extensive learning in law, history, science, philosophy, and literature. By his skill in the handling of the materials and by the force of his alert active mind he gives liveliness and vigour to a subject which, in other hands, might well be dull. Though he treats of the past as well as of the present, he so breathes the spirit of social needs and human justice into the past that to us, who read, it is the living present. Nothing seems dead; nothing seems past. We have the feeling of being present when the Sun God hands the code, ready made, to Hammurabi. If we ask ourselves why the past ages of the law are thus visualized and made present to our gaze, not only in this book but also in Dr Pound's other writings, we shall find one special reason to be his enthusiasm in the cause of justice. This is the key-note. Always looking upon enthusiasm as one of the greatest of powers, Madame de Staël says in *Corinne* that she recognizes only two really distinct classes of men—those who possess the capacity for enthusiasm and those who despise it. It is Dr Pound's capacity for enthusiasm which transforms the past into the present, giving it life and vigour.

The framework of the book is so designed as to permit a survey of thought from earlier to later times. In the words of Lord Morley, "a survey of this kind shows us in a clear and definite manner the various lines of road along which thinkers have travelled, and the point to which the subject has been brought in our own time. We are able to contrast methods and to compare their fruits. People always understand their own speculative position the better, the more clearly they are acquainted with the other positions which have been taken in the same matter." This is Dr Pound's method. He summarizes the work of the various schools of juridical thought from antiquity to our own time. He appraises the results attained by each one of these schools, and he criticizes these results from the standpoint of one whose scholarly gaze surveys the whole field of history and theory. He marks the permanent gains of each movement of legal thought; he suggests the ways in which these contributions to jurisprudential science may be fruitfully applied to social needs by the legislatures and courts of today. But Dr Pound does more than this. His book is not merely a history and a criticism of thought in regard to the processes and ends of legal growth; it is, at the same time, an expression of certain aspects of his own original thinking about law and legal history. From several points of view the most valuable feature of the book is the author's own theory as to the modes of legal progress and his own high conception of the part that the jurist should play in the making of law. The book is not only narrative and critical; it is also constructive. The wise student will reflect long upon the teaching of the master; and, whether he be convinced or not, his thoughts will never run fully in their old grooves.

Owing to its extensive survey of legal history and of juristic and philosophical thought in regard to legal history, Dr Pound's volume holds its own special place in this series of *Cambridge Studies in English Legal History*. In the design of the series, English legal history, viewed as the history of the law of England and of the many regions outside England which have inherited or adopted their legal institutions from England, forms a constituent, a vital, part of the history of Western civilization. Throughout all the stages of this evolution of English law as a world-system the relations with other legal systems have been close; and, from the days of Bracton to our own time, the ideas of English jurists as to the nature of law and the processes and ends of legal development have been intimately connected with the broader aspects of Western thought. One of the reasons why one prizes Dr Pound's book is that it shows us clearly these inter-relations between the ideas of English and the ideas of foreign jurists. The history of the speculations of English jurists is an integral part of the history of English law; but, in order that it may be properly understood, the history of English ideas in regard to law must be set out in its wider environment of European movements in philosophical and jurisprudential thought. As is natural to the jurist who inherits the traditions of the common law of England and America, Dr Pound devotes special attention to the history and principles of this system. But the jurist cannot restrict his study to one legal system alone; he must be familiar with many bodies of law and with the several stages of their history. He must possess a basis of comparison, a foundation for his conclusions as to the more general aspects of law and of the forces and principles which underlie the growth, spread, and decay of law. Dr Pound's learning in Germanic and Roman Law, his knowledge of the modern systems formed in large measure of these two legal elements, and his familiarity with Eastern law and primitive custom, have fitted him in a very special way for the difficult task of viewing

our Anglo-American jurisprudence in its wider environment of
Western development. He deals with the law and the juristic
thought of England and America and with their history; but he
sees and explains the connections with the world of law and of
theory outside England and outside America. It is the breadth
of view in *Interpretations of Legal History* which makes this
book particularly valuable as a contribution to studies concerned
with the history of English law in its world-wide aspects.

To the one accustomed to think in terms of insularity—to
regard the evolution of English legal rules and legal theories as
the sole and exclusive creation of the people in a small sea-girt
isle, a creation unconnected with the legal world outside and
beyond—Dr Pound's survey will come indeed as a revelation.
If the student of English law sincerely desires to view his subject, both historically and theoretically, in its wider aspects, he
will learn many lessons from this book—from the vastness of
its scope, its historical and philosophical range, its penetration
to fields of legal life and thought in different ages, its co-ordina-
tion of separate but related lines of legal growth and theory.
There is just as truly a world-wide commerce in juristic ideas
as there is a world-wide commerce in the goods produced by
economic industry; and this commerce in the concepts of
jurisprudence, this diffusion of the modes and results of thinking
about the history and the purposes of law, knows no frontiers
of land or sea. It is commerce borne from age to age and from
region to region by many forms of conveyance. The world-wide
movement of men and of books means the world-wide movement of thought. By such processes throughout the centuries
many of the legal ideas of today, in England and in other
civilized countries, have their origin with the civilians and
canonists and theologians of the middle age and the philosophers
and jurists of ancient Greece and Rome; the intellectual commerce of history has brought the juridical ideas of ancient and
medieval times to our modern shores. The speculations of a
Kant and a Hegel about right and justice, speculations passing
from book to book and from teacher to teacher, influence and
even determine the nature of legislation, judicial decisions, and
legal theories in scattered regions of the world where the very

names of the philosophers are unknown. Throughout her history
England has been on certain of the trade routes of this carriage
of jurisprudential ideas to and fro among the legal regions of the
world. English law and English thinking about law possess
indeed certain individual characteristics of their own; but those
very characteristics are blended of many diverse elements
derived from various sources. They are not purely indigenous,
purely racial, purely insular. There are features of English
jurisprudential thought which are truly insular; but, at the same
time, there are other features which are just as truly the common
heritage of England and of all the other regions of the West.
Even recent English schools of legal science—the analytical
and the historical schools, for example—are intimately related
to the ideas of Continental scholars. Austin and Maine are but
representatives of aspects of European thought. The commerce
in juridical ideas has known no frontiers.

   Such are some of the broader reflections which are induced
by the reading of Dr Pound's inspiring volume. But the book
embodies also certain other definite teachings. Thus, we find
that many aspects of English legal history are illumined for us
by the light of juristic interpretation: we catch new glimpses of
processes of legal growth from the time of the Anglo-Saxons
down through the epochs of Glanvill, Bracton, Coke, Mansfield,
and Eldon to our own day. Particularly instructive, also, are the
references to the common law as it has spread to America; and
there is here a rich field for the juristic comparison of the
common law in its old and in its new homes. The influence of
philosophical speculation upon the growth of English law in the
several periods of its history also stands out clearly: we can see
that Aristotle and Kant and Hegel have affected not only the
law itself, but also the attitude of the jurist toward the law.
Another special feature of the book is the author's criticism of
the English analytical and historical schools of jurisprudence.
The views of these schools have so firmly entrenched themselves
in the English mind that Dr Pound's acute and reasoned criticism—a criticism both destructive and constructive—will be
read with far more than ordinary interest. The whole volume,
in fact, lifts the mind out of some of its beaten tracks and places

it in newer paths. In the final chapter—"An Engineering Interpretation"—the author's own theory of legal history finds its fuller and more definite statement: and the one who accepts Dr Pound's teaching as to the processes of legal development and the ends of law will find himself regarding in a new light certain of the methods and the dogmas of the analytical and historical schools. Dr Pound's enlightened conception of the jurist's office is, again, one of the valuable contributions which he makes to juridical science. To him the jurist is—or at least ought to be—a creative and moulding force in legal progress.

The whole of Dr Pound's book is, in fact, a summoning of jurists to take their proper place of leadership in the work of adapting old law and creating new law to meet the ever-changing needs of social justice. The deadening effect of one of the teachings of the historical school of jurists—the teaching that law may be found, but not made—has too long kept jurists in their cloistered retreats. If they hearken to the lesson taught by Dr Pound, that law is made and re-made by men, and if they agree with him as to the nature of the jurist's function, they will take their own part in the legal life of society; they will apply their learning and their juristic statesmanship, consciously and continuously, to the reform of the law by influencing legislation and judicature and the other processes of law-making. Released from the fetters forged by the genius of Savigny, the legal historian will approach his materials with greater freedom of mind and more enlightened appreciation of the value of his studies. He will have his eye upon the present as well as upon the past; he will be able to make his histories of legal growth actual factors in the shaping of the law to meet present social needs. The study of legal history serves more than one purpose. If it has its uses in training and informing the mind, it has its uses also in guiding the activities of courts and legislatures. Legal history has a social function to fulfil. The historian of law is himself—or, rather, he may make of himself, if he will—a true statesman.

The Abbé Gratry, distinguished as the "Vico of the nineteenth century," deserves to be kept in remembrance: his *La Morale et la Loi de l'Histoire* is a valuable contribution to the philosophy of history. "Humanity hitherto passive now begins," says Gratry, "with full knowledge and entire freedom, to take into its hands the management of the affairs of the world; it enters into its age of manhood." In such an age legal traditions, unduly fostered and strengthened by the application of the tenets of Savigny and his school of historical jurists, need to be re-examined in the light of the newer social facts and forces of our day. Juristic thought has long been tending, in fact, in this direction. Maitland himself taught the doctrine that the historical spirit is not hostile to reform, that history is studied in order that progress may be made, in order that the past may not paralyse the present. The same ideas are taught by other legal historians. Even the question as to whether the judge is to be bound by precedents is being raised. "*Stare decisis,* as an absolute dogma," writes Dr Wigmore in his *Problems of Law,* "has seemed to me an unreal fetich....We possess all the detriment of uncertainty, which *stare decisis* was supposed to avoid, and also all the detriment of ancient law-lumber, which *stare decisis* concededly involves—the government of the living by the dead, as Herbert Spencer has called it." The newer school of jurists—jurists, too, who are masters of legal history—takes over and adopts the saying of Thomas Jefferson that "the earth belongs in usufruct to the living;...the dead have neither rights nor power over it." Such ideas are already affecting legislation. From certain points of view the English Law of Property Act, 1922, is conceived in the spirit of these ideas: it is an effort to be free of part of the "ancient law-lumber."

If an introduction has been written, when none was needed, may not the stimulus of Dr Pound's book be the cause and the justification?

H. D. H.

September 5, 1922

AUTHOR'S PREFACE

THESE lectures are printed as they were delivered at Trinity College, Cambridge, in Lent Term, 1922, with addition of some notes partly by way of illustration and partly to assist any who may be interested in pursuing the subject more deeply.

A complete history of the science of law in the last century would treat of the survival of eighteenth-century philosophy of law in some phases of Continental thinking and in American constitutional law and of the rise of a neo-Rousseauist theory on the basis thereof; of the different movements in the nineteenth-century metaphysical school; of the rise of the social philosophical school on its philosophical side and of the philosophical and juristic pedigrees of the neo-scholasticism and the revived natural law of the present century. It would trace the beginnings in nineteenth-century thought of the psychological and logical movements in recent philosophy of law. It would trace the relation of eighteenth-century natural law, as it survived in the nineteenth century, and of the metaphysical-historical jurisprudence of the latter century to juristic economic realism and to what might be called orthodox socialist jurisprudence. On another side it would identify the elements that went to make up the analytical school, would show the influence of that school on the one hand upon English historical jurisprudence and on the other hand upon the earlier sociological jurisprudence, and would show its connection with the social utilitarianism of today. On still another side it would trace the philosophical and juristic pedigree of the mechanical sociological jurisprudence of the nineteenth century and show how, following the progress of the social sciences, the sociological jurisprudence of today developed from that narrow and at first sight unpromising beginning. But the chief thread of this story would be the rise, the hegemony and the downfall of the historical school. Such a history would show how the natural-law thinking of the seventeenth and eighteenth centuries had already split into two channels in the latter part of the eighteenth century and split still further into three and ultimately four or five in the nineteenth century. It would show how these smaller streams of juristic thought began to converge at the end of that century and have been gathering more and more into two main channels in the present century. But it would show also, when the historian looked back over the whole course, that during the last century on the whole the historical school represented the main stream. A history of the rise and the decay of the historical school founded by Savigny would not be the whole of the history of juristic thought in the nineteenth century. But it would be the core and the largest part of such a history. The schools of today have arisen out of the dissolution of Savigny's school almost as definitely as the schools of the last century grew out of the dissolution of the law-of-nature school. Its influence on the law and the legal thinking of today is as palpable as the influence of the law-of-nature school on the law and the legal thinking of the first half of the nineteenth century.

Only a small part of the lesser task is within the scope of the present lectures. They do not essay even a history of the historical jurisprudence of the nineteenth century. They have to do with one aspect thereof only, namely, the way in which the historical school understood legal history and the relation of its interpretations to the purposes of the time. Moreover the design is not to tell a bit of juristic history as such but to consider the modes of thought of the historical school and its derivatives as an element in the legal science of today, to appraise their value for present purposes, and to look into the possibilities of other interpretations which the nineteenth-century historical school rejected or ignored. Yet one cannot do these things without treating the nineteenth-century interpretations of legal history as part of the history of juristic thought in that century and in their relations to all the currents in which it ran.

My chief obligation is to Senator Benedetto Croce. His writings which were of special use to me are cited in the notes.

In addition I had the privilege of talking with him about the subject while the lectures were writing. I must also express my grateful appreciation of the hospitality and courtesy of the teachers of law at Cambridge and of the Master and Fellows of Trinity College, which made my brief stay with that company of scholars something always to be remembered.

R. P.

SQUIRE LAW LIBRARY,
    CAMBRIDGE,
        May 4, 1922.

CONTENTS

I

LAW AND HISTORY

LAW must be stable and yet it cannot stand still. Hence all thinking about law has struggled to reconcile the conflicting demands of the need of stability and of the need of change. The social interest in the general security has led men to seek some fixed basis for an absolute ordering of human action whereby a firm and stable social order might be assured. But continual changes in the circumstances of social life demand continual new adjustments to the pressure of other social interests as well as to new modes of endangering security. Thus the legal order must be flexible as well as stable. It must be overhauled continually and refitted continually to the changes in the actual life which it is to govern. If we seek principles, we must seek principles of change no less than principles of stability. Accordingly the chief problem to which legal thinkers have addressed themselves has been how to reconcile the idea of a fixed body of law, affording no scope for individual wilfulness, with the idea of change and growth and making of new law; how to unify the theory of law with the theory of making law and to unify the system of legal justice with the facts of administration of justice by magistrates.

For, put more concretely, the problem of compromise between the need of stability and the need of change becomes in one aspect a problem of adjustment between rule and discretion, between administering justice according to settled rule, or at most by rigid deduction from narrowly fixed premises, and administration of justice according to the more or less trained intuition of experienced magistrates. In one way or another almost all of the vexed questions of the science of law prove to be phases of this same problem. In the last century the great battles of the analytical and the historical jurists were waged over the question of the nature of law—whether the traditional or the imperative element of legal systems was to be taken as the type of law—and over the related questions as to the nature of law-making—whether law is found by judges and jurists or is made to order by conscious law-givers—and as to the basis of the law's authority—whether it lies in reason and science or in command and sovereign will. But the whole significance of these questions lies in their bearing upon the problem of adjustment between or reconciliation of rule and discretion, or, as it is ultimately, the problem of stability and change—of the general security and the individual human life. And so it is with the philosophical problems of jurisprudence and with the most debated practical problems of law. When we discuss the relation of law and morals or the distinction between law and equity, or the respective provinces of court and jury, or the advisability of fixed rules or of wide judicial power in procedure, or the much-debated question as to judicial sentence or administrative individualization in the treatment of criminals, at bottom we have to do with forms of the same fundamental problem[1].

Attempts to unify or to reconcile stability and change, to make the legal order appear something fixed and settled and beyond question, while at the same time allowing adaptation to the pressure of infinite and variable human desires, have proceeded along three main lines—authority, philosophy, and history. The Greek and Roman world relied upon authority and later upon philosophy. The modern world has relied successively upon authority, upon philosophy and upon history —roughly speaking, upon authority from the twelfth century to the sixteenth, upon philosophy during the seventeenth and eighteenth centuries, and upon history during the nineteenth century. But none of these disappear when the next comes into favour. In the reign of philosophy we get a philosophical authority alongside of and overshadowing authority as such. In the reign of history we find a historical authority and a historical philosophy alongside of intrinsic authority and philosophical authority and overshadowing both.

---

[1] I have developed this proposition in detail in a paper entitled "Theories of Law," 22 *Yale Law Journal*, 114.

In its earliest form the idea of authority appears as belief in a divinely ordained or divinely dictated body of rules, as in Hammurabi's code, handed him by the Sun-god ready made, or the Mosaic law, or the laws of Manu, dictated to the sages by Manu's son in Manu's presence and by his direction. In its latest form it is a dogma that law is a body of commands of the sovereign power in a politically organized society, resting ultimately on whatever basis is conceived to be behind the capacity of that sovereign. Such was the doctrine of the Roman jurists of the Republic with respect to the strict law, and as the emperor wielded by devolution all the legal powers of the Roman people, it could be laid down as a legal proposition that the will of the emperor had the force of law. This way of thinking was congenial to the lawyers who took the side of royal authority in sixteenth- and seventeenth-century France and through them passed into the doctrine of modern public law. After 1688 it was readily adjustable to Coke's dogma of the omnipotence of Parliament, now become a political verity, and became the orthodox English theory. Also when at the American Revolution and later at the French Revolution "the people" were thought of as succeeding to the sovereignty of the British Parliament or of the French king, it was easily made to fit a conception of popular sovereignty. In any of these forms it puts a single ultimate unchallengeable author behind the legal order and as the source of every legal precept, whose declared will is binding simply as such. It asserts that all the rules which are actually applied in the administration of justice proceed from that source mediately or immediately. It conceives of interpretation as a simple process of ascertaining an actually existent intent of the author of the precept and of application as a purely mechanical process of an infallible legal logic in which it is wholly immaterial for the result who happens to be the interpreter or who happens to make the application or wherefore he is called upon to interpret or to apply. In place of the nature-god or religious god of primitive codes it sets up a political god in the form of State or People. For in this mode of thinking men have their eyes upon the need of stability more than upon the need of change. Usually they deny that law

1—2

changes or at least conveniently fail to see that changes are
going on incessantly below the surface. From time to time they
make the inevitable readjustments by alteration of the recorded
revelation, by interpretations that leave the letter intact but
give the text a wholly new meaning, by fictions often comparable to the "let's play" this or that of children, or by a more
subtle fiction of new authoritative divine pronouncements
declaratory of the old. When fully conscious of change and
driven to seek a fixed and absolute basis therefor, the believer
in authority postulates deliberate and avowed special creation
or new revelation by his political god.

When, for a time, the need of change comes to hold the first
place in men's eyes, as a result of wide and rapid political or
commercial or industrial expansion, they turn to philosophy.
For if the most rigid of codes demands "interpretation" and
"application," with all the adaptations which those terms affect
to conceal, and so is made to accommodate itself to the fluidity
of life, yet the most rapid legal growth or expansion does not
permit the lawyer to ignore the demand for stability. The call
for a theory of an ultimate and unchallengeable source is replaced by the need of a directing and organizing theory whereby
the growth of law may be compatible with the maintenance of
the general security. In practice the change or growth takes
place by application of some new technique to the old materials
or by joining old materials more or less reshaped to new ones
found outside of the law. Commonly the process is chiefly one
of analogical development of the old materials by extension here
and restriction there, by generalization, and by cautious striking
out of new paths, paved in part at least with old materials but
given a new direction by trial and error. Such a process may
easily disturb the general security, as may be seen in the earlier
days of English equity and in the legal history of more than one
American commonwealth in the formative stage of its institutions. Maintenance of the general security requires something
to fix the new technique, to mark the lines of the reshaping, to
guide the analogical extensions and restrictions and to provide
limits for the process of trial and error. Both in the classical
Roman law and in the analogous period in modern law, the

seventeenth and eighteenth centuries, this need was met by philosophy in the form of the theory of a law of nature.

In fact jurist or text-writer or judge or legislator, working under the theory of natural law, measured all situations and sought to solve all difficulties by referring them to an idealized picture of the social order of the time and place and a conception of the end of law in terms of that social order. In effect he sought so to shape or so to construct legal institutions and legal precepts that the legal order should maintain and further this ideal. But while this idealizing of the social order as it was sufficed in practice to enable him to go forward with due regard to the general security, it did not seem a sufficient guarantee. It did not satisfy his desire for a perfect law which should stand fast for ever, such as the idea of authority had pictured it, nor did it suffice to prove to mankind at large that law rested upon something more stable than human will, more constant than human desire to do justice, and more to be relied upon than human ingenuity, and hence might claim complete and unquestioning obedience. Accordingly the ideal of the social order was taken to be the ultimate reality of which legal institutions and rules and doctrines were but reflections or declarations. True, it was not put in this way. The theory was that natural law was that which expressed perfectly the idea of law, that a rule of natural law was one which expressed perfectly the idea of law applied to the matter in hand, and that positive law got its whole validity from this natural law which it reflected and declared. But the idea of law, on which everything turned, was a juristic idealization of the social order of the time and place.

Primarily the theory of natural law as a juristic doctrine was a theory of making law. The old materials were to be tested by the ideal and were to be reshaped to conform to it or, if this was not possible, were to be rejected. If there were gaps to be filled, they were to be filled in conformity with the ideal plan. Yet it tended to become also a theory of law because of pressure of the interest in the general security. Thus it happened presently that a new authority was set up thereby—a philosophical authority of the "nature of things" or of the "nature of man."

Once more the legal order was the revelation of a god. The new juristic god was called "reason," and was represented as hostile to authority. But his hostility extended only to the authority of gods other than himself. Once the legal world had been made over in his image the lines were to be as rigid and the legal structures as firmly fixed and the doctrines as unbending as under the reign of nature gods or religious gods or political gods. For the philosophical revelation extended only to an ideal picture of society. The details were filled in by lawyers, chiefly from the materials of the law which had been taught them, and once filled in got all the authorIty of the ideal plan. American constitutional law is full of examples of common-law dogmas made over to fit the ideal conception of the "nature of American institutions" and thus fixed as items of natural law beyond the reach of legislative change.

Nevertheless the philosophical reconciliation of stability and change was a notable advance in that, if it put the plan beyond the reach of human law-givers, it called for continual scrutiny of the building in all its details in order to be assured that they conformed to the plan. Thus it took account of changes in the positive law as such. Moreover, while the plan when found was eternal and immutable, it was to be found by reason and it was always arguable that what had been taken for the one authentic plan was but an imperfect approximation. While legal systems were freely absorbing materials from without, as in the development of equity and the taking over of the law merchant in English law, the theory of natural law served well. But when the absorption was complete for the time being and stability required a pause to assimilate fully what had been taken up during the period of growth and called for internal ordering and harmonizing and systematizing rather than for creation, it ceased to satisfy. A reconciliation in terms of stability rather than in terms of change was demanded and this reconciliation was effected through history.

In law, as in everything else, the nineteenth century is the century of history. As every eighteenth-century decision and treatise and statute presupposes philosophy of law and is *pro tanto* consciously or unconsciously a bit of philosophical exposition, so every nineteenth-century decision and treatise and in its interpretation and application, if not in its very conception and enactment, every nineteenth-century statute presupposes legal history and, as the culmination of a bit of history, involves consciously or unconsciously an interpretation thereof. Hence we must not confine ourselves to professed historians of law, important as they are for our purpose. We must take account of the whole body of legal literature—decisions, juristic writing and legislation. For in the nineteenth century ideas of history and of the interpretation of history were at work throughout the law and throughout legal literature.

There was a fundamental contrast in this respect with the legal literature of the past. The short history of Roman law by Pomponius, preserved in the Digest, is no more than an interesting exordium to a dogmatic sketch of Roman law. It gives us the names of the men who had set up the several institutions of the Roman legal order, sets forth by whom the chief authoritative enactments were proposed, and tells us the names of the jurists who, by their *responsa* and their teachings and their writings, declared and made known the principles involved in the nature of things as applied to legal controversies. Not a line of what follows would have been different if this exordium were omitted or were written otherwise from end to end. So likewise with the somewhat apologetic preface with which Gaius begins his exposition of the Twelve Tables. Why should one, he asks in effect, begin a commentary on Roman legislation with the founding of the city? So far as the preliminary historical survey is more than an exordium—and he expressly justifies it on rhetorical grounds as such—it is an incident of the philosophical attitude. A thing is perfect only when complete in all its parts and the beginning of anything is an essential part. Hence the natural or ideal exposition must include history [1]. The teachers and students of Roman law from the twelfth to the fifteenth century did not think of that law as a bit of history

---

[1] "In setting out to expound the ancient laws, it has seemed right as of course to go back to the founding of the city for my account of the law of the Roman people, not because I would write needlessly verbose commentaries but because I notice that in all matters a thing is perfect only when it is complete in all its parts, and certainly the beginning is the most essential

but as authority. As the declared will of Justinian, whose successors still sat in the seat of Augustus, it was a living authoritative system. To them there was no question of history but only of interpretation and application of a binding text. The legal history of Cujas, who has been spoken of as a precursor of the historical school, is a Humanist reconstruction of classical antiquity, as a part of the intellectual movement of the time, not an attempt to put historically found principles on the throne of Justinian. Even the historical research of Conring, for which much has been claimed[1], is no more than a pulling down of what had passed for that throne by showing that it was not the genuine seat of Augustus and Justinian after philosophy had replaced authority and the dogma of the legal and political continuity of the Empire had ceased to matter.

English legal history-writing prior to the nineteenth century is more closely related to the legal history of that century in that it is nationalist, and has an immediate practical purpose of setting up a historical authority as a basis for the legal order. Fortescue writes a historical sketch to show that England had always been governed by the same customs from pre-Roman Britain. He could not claim the authority of Justinian nor of any other sovereign law-giver for the unwritten common law of England. But the "written law" laid down that immemorial custom had authority as well as, and in the absence of, written laws, and the common law of England was shown by history to be the body of rules by which Englishmen had always been wont to adjudge controversies and to guide their conduct. Coke's Second Institute is a history of public law in which he seeks to make out the case of the common-law courts against the Stuart kings by setting forth the immemorial common-law rights of Englishmen, possessed by their forefathers from the beginning and declared by Magna Carta, by a long succession

part of anything. Moreover, if it is monstrous, as it were, for one who is arguing a cause in the forum to lay out his case to the judge without some preliminary statement, how much more is it unsuitable for one who expounds to disregard the beginning and omit historical causes and take up the subject matter to be expounded, if one may say so, at once with unwashed hands." Gaius (on the Law of the Twelve Tables, 1), *Digest*, 1, 2, 1.

[1] Stobbe, *Hermann Conring, Der Begründer der deutschen Rechtsgeschichte* (1870).

of statutes, and by a long and continuous succession of judicial decisions. The premises are the same as Fortescue's and the method is that of the advocate. The purpose is not to find a basis for authority but to identify authority. In Hale, also, with his proposition that the origins of English law are as undiscoverable as the sources of the Nile, we have the same idea of a historical identification of authority, although there is a suggestion of a combination of philosophy and history in a period of philosophical hegemony which reminds us of Gaius. Finally Blackstone, at the height of the reign of philosophy, reconciles stability and change by adopting the historical theory of continuity of an immemorial custom, as expounded by Fortescue, Coke, and Hale, and adding a doctrine of change by authority of Parliament, in terms of Coke and of the Revolution of 1688; unifying the two ideas by the philosophical theory of a law of nature of which each was declaratory and conformity whereto gave to each its ultimate validity.

Nineteenth-century legal history-writing had a radically different purpose. It did not think of a law which had always been the same but of a law which had grown. It sought stability through establishment of principles of growth, finding the lines along which growth had proceeded and would continue to proceed, and it sought to unify stability and change by a combination of historical authority and philosophical history. Utilizing the idea of authority, it sought to put a historical foundation under the seventeenth- and eighteenth-century theory of law as only declaratory of something having a higher authority than the pronouncement of legislator or judge as such. Law was not declaratory of morals or of the nature of man as a moral entity or reasoning creature. It was declaratory of principles of progress discovered by human experience of administering justice and of human experience of intercourse in civilized society; and these principles were not principles of natural law revealed by reason, they were realizings of an idea, unfolding in human experience and in the development of institutions—an idea to be demonstrated metaphysically and verified by history. All of this body of doctrine did not develop at once. But such was the creed of the school which was dominant in the science of law throughout the century and in one form or another this creed may be identified in all the varieties of juristic thinking during the century, even in schools which professed a different method.

After flourishing for a hundred years and ruling almost un-contested during the latter half of that period, the historical school came into marked disfavour at the end of the nineteenth century and broke down as completely at the beginning of the present century as the law-of-nature school had broken down at the end of the eighteenth century. As early as 1888 Stammler made a formidable philosophical attack upon it in his *Methode der geschichtlichen Rechtswissenschaft*, followed up in his well-known books of 1896 and 1902. In the latter year a leading exponent of the historical school in France accused it of "ab-dicating" and of leading to legal immobility and gave what proved a decisive impetus to the so-called revival of natural law in that country[1]. In 1897 Mr Justice Holmes, who had done notable work in the historical interpretation of Anglo-American law in the hey-day of the school, criticized its habitual failure to take conscious account of the considerations of social advantage on which rules of law must be justified, its negative attitude with respect to improvement of the law, and its rooted tendency to hold a rule wholly established as a suitable or even necessary rule of action today if it could but be shown that it obtained in embryo or in historical principle in the Year Books[2]. Some of the historical school went over to positivism. Others turned to the economic interpretation of legal history, or to historical materialism. Others asserted that a distinction must be made "between history and the historical school," gave up historical jurisprudence, and confined themselves to a purely descriptive legal history and a purely descriptive teaching of law[3]. Finally Kohler, who had done great things in historical jurisprudence, turned to philosophy and in his neo-Hegelian

[1] Saleilles, "L'École historique et droit naturel," *Revue trimestrielle de droit civil*, I, 90, 94 (1902).
[2] "The Path of the Law," 10 *Harvard Law Review*, 457, 467 (1907); *Collected Papers*, p. 184.
[3] Saleilles, *Le code civil et la méthode historique*, Livre du centenaire du code civil, I, 99 (1904).

philosophical jurisprudence insisted upon the element of creative activity, upon the adapting of the legal materials of the past, shaped by and adapted to the civilizations of the past, to the exigencies of civilization in the present and the requirements of a continually changing and moving civilization[1]. Indeed, this break-up of the historical school coincides with a general abandonment of the nineteenth-century historico-philosophical thinking in every field and the revival of faith in the efficacy of human effort with an accompanying call for philosophies of action and of creation in place of the political fatalism and juristic pessimism of the immediate past. All this was observable before the war, but the war gave it added impetus. For it demonstrated the rôle which human initiative, half blind, erroneous, misdirected as it may be, does play in the building of institutions and the shaping of human events; it visibly overturned the social and psychological foundations of nineteenth-century thought, already undermined but still standing. All the nineteenth-century schools were agreed upon the futility of conscious action, although for different reasons. They conceived of a slow and ordered succession of events and of institutions whereby things perfected themselves by evolving to the limit of their idea. Just as clearly all the recent philosophies of every type are philosophies of action.

Pragmatism sees validity in actions, not in that they realize the idea, but to the extent that they are effective for their purpose and in purposes to the extent that they satisfy a maximum of human demands. Bergson's intuitionism shows us how we act better than we know and achieve results by trial and error to meet human desires which we explain to ourselves by ideas. The implication is that we need not fear to act. Historical scepticism, in contrast with ancient scepticism, which taught men not to act, teaches action by attacking the dogma of historical fatalism and the doctrine that what does not exist in historical idea is an idle hope. Activist idealism reaches a result directly opposite to the conclusion of the idealism of the past, which regarded the man who acted as a vain disturber of the rational and foreordained order. The relativisms that are

[1] *Rechtsphilosophie und Universalrechtsgeschichte*, § 8 (1904).

springing up on every hand are, on their practical side, philosophies of action with respect to something desired. Croce's
identification of philosophy and history rejects the nineteenth-
century philosophy of history and is a philosophy of life with
all its variety and action and change and compromise and
adaptation. When men are thinking thus a functional attitude
in jurisprudence is inevitable. Nor is this way of thinking merely
the natural and temporary attitude of those who have been
actors in or spectators of the far-reaching changes of the past
decade. It grows out of the need for action to meet the pressure
of new demands consequent upon changes in the social order
and of new desires both behind and involved in those changes.
As the theory of the law of nature came in as one of growth and
of creation, to take better account of the element of change in
the reconciliation of stability and change, and ended in assuming
that the one key to reason had been found for all time and that
social and legal and political charts had been drawn up by which
men and law-makers and peoples might be guided forever, so,
it may be, the historical theory, which sought a new reconciliation
in an idea of growth and progress, had come to deny growth
and progress in any effective sense through its belief that it
had discovered finally the immutable lines of growth or had
calculated once for all the fixed orbit of progress outside of
which no movement could possibly take place.

We may well believe, then, that an epoch in juristic thought
has come to an end, and that the time is ripe to appraise its
work, to ask what of permanent value it has achieved, to inquire
what are the present demands which it is unable to satisfy, and
to consider wherein its way of unifying stability and change,
with which men were content for a century, is no longer of
service.

To understand the juristic creed of the historical school of
the last century we must bear in mind that it was a passive
restraining mode of thought on legal subjects by way of reaction
from the active, creative juristic thought of the era of philosophy. Nor is this all. More immediately it was a reaction
from two phases of the natural-law thinking in its last stage,
namely from the paper-constitution making and confident dis-

regard of traditional political institutions and conditions of time and place which characterized the era of the French Revolution and from the belief in the power of reason to work miracles in legislation and consequent no less confident code-making of the end of the eighteenth and beginning of the nineteenth century. Writing to Madison in 1789, Jefferson had said that the earth belonged "in usufruct to the living," that in consequence every constitution and every law naturally expired at the end of nineteen years, and that if enforced longer, it was imposed by force and not by right. Proceeding on the political doctrine of the consent of the governed, he argued that every new generation should renew that consent which gives to law its binding force and that unless this consent was so renewed as to each rule of law the rule ceased to be obligatory[1]. As has been shown more than once, Burke, in reaction from such ideas of the era of the French Revolution, was feeling in political science for the ideas which the historical school afterwards made current in jurisprudence[2]. Fourteen years before

[1] "I set out on this ground which I suppose to be self evident, 'that the earth belongs in usufruct to the living,' that the dead have neither powers nor rights over it....On similar grounds it may be proved that no society can make a perpetual constitution or even a perpetual law. The earth belongs always to the living generation. They may manage it then, and what proceeds from it, during their usufruct. They are masters, too, of their own persons, and consequently may govern them as they please. But persons and property make the sum of the objects of government. The constitution and the laws of their predecessors extinguished them, in their natural course, with those whose will gave them being. This could preserve that being till it ceased to be itself, and no longer. Every constitution, then, and every law, naturally expires at the end of 19 years." Letter to James Madison, September 6, 1789, Jefferson's *Writings* (Ford's edition), v, 115–116, 121.

"It is now forty years since the constitution of Virginia was formed. The same tables inform us, that, within that period, two thirds of the adults then living are now dead. Have then the remaining third, even if they have the wish, the right to hold in obedience to their will, and to laws heretofore made by them, the other two-thirds, who, with themselves, compose the present mass of adults? If they have not, who has? The dead? But the dead have no rights. They are nothing; and nothing cannot own something. Where there is no substance, there can be no accident. This corporeal globe, and everything upon it, belong to its present corporeal inhabitants, during their generation. They alone have a right to direct what is the concern of themselves alone, and to declare the law of that direction; and this declaration can only be made by their majority." Letter to Samuel Kerchevall, July 12, 1816, *Id.* x, 43–44.

[2] "Society is indeed a contract. Subordinate contracts for objects of mere occasional interest may be dissolved at pleasure—but the State ought

Savigny's memorable tract they were set forth for political history by Cuoco[1]. Indeed it seems to have been shown that Burke's *Reflections on the Revolution in France* had a direct influence upon Savigny[2].

But chiefly Savigny's doctrine was a reaction from the legislative theory of the law-of-nature school in the period of legislation and codification with which the reign of philosophy came to an end. It was believed that the jurist, by a mere effort of reason, might frame a perfect code which could be administered by judges mechanically as ultimate legal wisdom. Under the influence of this idea men were scornful of history and of traditional legal materials. All that was required might be done by unaided reason as if there had never been a legal past. The one thing needful was to draft into service the most powerful reason in the state, obtain a perfect code through the exercise of this reason, and hold down inferior reasons to its text[3]. Such was the theory—though happily by no means always the practice —of the Code of Frederick the Great, of which the first draft was published in 1749 (though the code was not completed and put in force till 1780–1794), of the Austrian code, projected in 1713, begun in 1767 and put in force in 1811, and of the French civil code, begun in 1800, put in force in 1804 and copied freely throughout the world during the nineteenth century[4]. It was a result of the natural-law philosophy, of the extreme scope for personal opinion to which that philosophy led, especially in

not to be considered as nothing better than a partnership agreement in a trade of pepper and coffee, calico or tobacco, or some other low concern, to be taken up for a little temporary interest, and to be dissolved by the fancy of the parties." *Reflections on the Revolution in France, Works* (1839 edition), III, 118 (1790).

[1] *Saggio storico*, §§ 1–7 (1800).

[2] See Braune, *Edmund Burke in Deutschland* (1917).

[3] Hence in the Code of Frederick the Great there was to be no judicial power of interpretation. The judges were to consult a royal commission as to any doubtful points and to be bound absolutely by its answer. *Prussian Landrecht*, Introduction, §§ 47–48. Compare French Civil Code, Art. 5; Savigny, *System des heutigen römischen Rechts*, I, § 31.

[4] "Men longed for new codes, which, by their completeness, should insure a mechanically precise administration of justice, so that the judge, relieved from the exercise of his own opinions, should be confined to bare literal application." Savigny, *Vom Beruf unsrer Zeit für Gesetzgebung und Rechtswissenschaft*, chap. 1 (1814), 2nd ed. p. 5.

its identification of law with morals, and of the rise of centralized absolute governments in Western Europe in the seventeenth and eighteenth centuries.

In his tract on the vocation of the age for legislation and jurisprudence, which marks the beginning of the historical school in law, Savigny manifestly attacks the three phases of eighteenth-century legal thought just described. But he attacks them as he saw them; particularly the results of the third in legal thinking as they had fused with the Byzantine conception of law, drawn from the *Corpus Juris* and handed down from the twelfth-century academic idea of the statutory authority of Roman law in the Western Europe of that time[1].

Savigny saw clearly the historical and doctrinal crudities[2] of the framers of the French civil code; so clearly, indeed, that he overlooked the extent to which their bad Roman law often was made to result in good French law. Thus, he has no difficulty in showing that they wholly misunderstood and misstated the Roman law of usucapion with respect to stolen property[3]. But the rule which they laid down (really taken from the customary law of the north of France) was infinitely better for a commercial and industrial society than the actual Roman law, based on conditions in the old city of Rome. The fact that the rule which they adopted, mistakenly supposing it to be Roman law, has won its way in all Roman-law countries and is making

[1] "[The call for a code] is related to many projects and attempts of the sort since the middle of the eighteenth century. At this time the whole of Europe was moved by a blind enthusiasm for improvement. All sense of the importance of other times, of the natural development of societies and institutions, and hence of all that is sound and worth while in history, had been lost. Its place was taken by extravagant expectations as to the possibilities of the present, which, it was believed, was to be nothing less than an ideal of perfection." *Ibid.* 2nd ed. pp. 6–7.

[2] "Such phenomena as Desquiron's speaking of a 'Roman jurist, one Justus Lipsius, soon after the Twelve Tables' and of 'the famous Sicardus under Theodosius Second, framer of the Theodosian Code' are significant." *Id.* chap. 7, 2nd ed. p. 61. Perhaps one need not say that Lipsius was a sixteenth-century Dutch Humanist and Sicardus (Sichard) a sixteenth-century French editor of the Theodosian Code.

[3] "In another place he [Maleville] speaks of the *usucapio* of Justinian. He says we must distinguish between the thief and the third person who buys from the thief; that the first requires thirty years, while the other is within the purview of *L. un. C. de usuc. transform.* and hence of the three years' prescription, as if the Romans had never heard of *res furtiva.*" *Ibid.*

greater headway continually in countries governed by English law speaks for itself. But it happened often that Savigny had a better case, as, for example, in the matter of civil death, where seventeenth-century French law had made a curious fusion of Germanic civil death through outlawry with Roman *capitis deminutio*, of which Revolutionary France had taken advantage as a weapon against the *émigrés*. The historical ignorance or indifference of the compilers of the code led them to codify the resulting mess and to put into the code a compound of primitive law, of the legislation of Louis XIV against the Huguenots, and of the legislation of Revolutionary France against the *émigrés*, which was much behind the law of Justinian[1]. It was this sort of codifying that made Savigny so sceptical as to the efficacy of conscious law-making.

Thus we may account for the characteristics of the school founded by Savigny when we look at the problems of jurisprudence in his time, the questions he was discussing and the purposes for which he discussed them. As its first tenet it held that law was found, not made; that is, it was a theory of the traditional element in modern law because the confident disregard of that element and belief that law might be made out of whole cloth by a sheer effort of juristic reason had led to the unworkable prohibitions upon judicial interpretation of the Prussian code, to the crude legislation as to extinction of personality which Savigny exposed at such length in his *System of the Modern Roman Law*, and to the legislation upon divorce which he dissects historically in his tract upon legislation and jurisprudence[2]. Yet there is more to be noted. In a wider sense this doctrine was a phase of a general reaction from the eighteenth-century idea of civilization as something produced

---

[1] *Jural Relations*, transl. by Rattigan, pp. 111–119.

[2] "On the subject of divorce the Roman law is cited continually. But Portalis and Maleville begin with a history of Roman divorce which is not merely false, it is wholly impossible. For example, they both believe that marriage could not be dissolved by one party but only by mutual consent, thus making the whole law of the Pandects on this subject and even the law of Justinian quite devoid of sense, and that divorce by mutual consent in Roman law is only a consequence of a mistaken doctrine that marriage rests upon the same basis as other contracts." *Vom Beruf unsrer Zeit für Gesetzgebung und Rechtswissenschaft*, chap. 7, 2nd ed. pp. 63–64.

ab extra by the action of a wise law-giver or by some inventive and master-spirited people[1]. Nor may we overlook the connection between the attitude of the historical school toward creative work in law and the circumstance that in contrast with the law-of-nature school of the seventeenth and eighteenth centuries it was a school of academic jurists. Savigny was a professor of law who gave up the chancellorship of Prussia to go back to his chair. Puchta was a professor. Maine's great work was done as a professor at Oxford and his administrative experience was the lesser part of his life. Ames and Thayer and Bigelow in America were professors of almost exclusively academic experience. Compare with them Grotius, whose career was wholly diplomatic and political; Montesquieu with a wholly political career; Vattel, whose activities were entirely diplomatic and political; Burlamaqui, whose teaching was a mere incident in a political career; Blackstone, whose lectures at Oxford were an episode in a career as lawyer and judge, and in America Kent and Story whose lives were spent chiefly in judicial office. Even Pufendorf and Wolff, whose main work was academic, both had stormy careers because they insisted on meddling with politics. It is not an accident that the one group conceived that law could only be found by historical study, distrusted legislation and were averse to action, while the other group conceived that they could construct schemes of natural law by exercise of their powers of reason, taught principles of constructive legislation and believed in action[2].

Secondly the historical school throughout its existence held to some form of idealistic interpretation of legal history. Savigny was unconsciously much under the influence of the ideas of the law-of-nature school in which he had been trained. He as-

[1] See Croce, *Storia della storiografia Italiana nel secolo decimonono*, I, 22–23.

[2] "The historical school came to exactly the opposite doctrine [from the law-of-nature school] because of a romantic disposition which found a contemplative immersion in history more attractive than actual taking part in the battles of the day, as successor of the hasty and somewhat crude pretentious codifications of the sanguine, action-loving era of the French Revolution, as citizen of a century of dormant political life, through the help of a complaisant metaphysic which asserted that it had found 'the reasonable' already worked out, and finally because of the learned tradition that confined it to the working over of a body of law traditionally received." Kantorowicz, *Zur Lehre vom richtigen Recht*, p. 8 (1909).

sumed the seventeenth- and eighteenth-century doctrine that law was only declaratory, and simply put a historical foundation under it in place of its original philosophical foundation. Nothing could have been better adapted to the demands of this new foundation for an old way of thinking than the Hegelian philosophy of history. An idea was realizing in legal history. It could be discovered by historical research and when discovered its implications could be developed logically. Thus history, philosophy and analysis, the three weapons in the jurist's armoury, could be used in conjunction in a science of law resting on the assured and stable foundation of fixed principles of historical development involved in the unfolding and progressive realization of the idea[1]. Metaphysics reinforced history by showing us the same idea as a fundamentally given datum[2]. Analysis supplemented history by enabling the jurist to work out the logical implications of the principles in which the idea was realized[3].

Third, the historical school insisted on the social pressure behind rules where the philosophical school of the preceding centuries had insisted on the intrinsic force of the just rule as binding upon a moral entity and the analytical school later insisted upon the force of politically organized society. If a given rule realized the idea, as it had unfolded in human experience of intercourse of men with men or of the administration of justice among men, conduct and adjudication would conform thereto as a matter of custom and nothing was required beyond judicial or juristic ascertainment and formulation thereof[4].

[1] "The complete science of law, therefore, consists in comprehending the whole of the conception of right as developed in time or, in other words, in universal history of right and law, that is, investigation of the perennial relation of legal development to the historical principle of the people and demonstration that the realities of right and law have developed organically in the course of time in the progress of history, and how this has taken place." Friedländer, *Juristische Encyklopädie*, p. 65 (1847).

[2] "Philosophical jurisprudence has for its subject the idea of right and law, that is the conception of right and law and its realization." Hegel, *Grundlinien der Philosophie des Rechts*, § 1 (1820).

[3] Hence, says Puchta, jurisprudence is "scientific knowledge of the history and system of law." *Cursus der Institutionen*, I, § 33 (1841).

[4] See, e.g., Clark, *Practical Jurisprudence*, p. 134 (1883); Maine, *International Law*, Lecture II (1888); Carter, *The Ideal and the Actual in Law*, pp. 10–11 (1890).

Nationalism was not a necessary nor was it an important item in the creed of this historical school[1]. Savigny's nationalism was partly inherited from the Protestant jurist-theologians of the sixteenth century, reinforced by the rise of strong central governments in the seventeenth and eighteenth centuries. But for the most part it was an incident of the reaction from the ideas and juristic methods of the French Revolution. As against the abstract propositions of natural law expressed in algebraic formulas in the Declaration of the Rights of Man, it called for ideas drawn from the very depths of the nation. In this respect it is comparable to the attitude of Burke toward these formulas in politics and of Cuoco towards them in political history. It was a protest against importation of the abstract ideas and formulas of the French Revolution without ability to import with them the conditions of fact in and out of which they arose[2]. But Savigny was a Romanist and his faith in the historically discovered Roman idea made his legal science quite as universal as that of the adherents of natural law. The Germanists, who found the idea through research exclusively within the old Germanic law, were the nationalist group of his school.

After a century of historical jurisprudence along these lines we have come to think that it was not a historical school at all. It assumed legal history as an absolutely given datum. It assumed progress as something for which a basis could be found within itself, as progress of reason or of the spirit or in the unfolding of the idea. It assumed that a single causal factor was at work in legal history and that some one idea would suffice to give a complete account of all legal phenomena. It laboured under what has been called the "illusion of perspective." For when we look at the rules or the decisions or the texts of the past, through a rationalized medium of legal analysis and system, in a different setting from that in which they took form and were applied, we look at them for the purposes of present problems and with the ideas and the setting of the

[1] But compare Vinogradoff, *Historical Jurisprudence*, I, 124–135 (1920), where the historical jurists are grouped as nationalists in distinction from rationalists and evolutionists.

[2] Croce, *Storia della storiografia Italiana nel secolo decimonono*, I, 11.

present before us. It by no means follows that what we see thus through the spectacles of the present is anything that was applied actually to the decision of causes anywhere or at any time. It is more likely to be an idealized reflection upon the legal problems of the present in terms of the texts of the past. Whenever we look back at law, when we look at anything beyond the actual course of judicature beneath our eyes, and for some purposes and in some relations even then, we must interpret. With the historical school the interpretation, or as Croce puts it the history-writing, passed for history.

In the course of the hegemony of the historical school many interpretations of legal history developed which both grew out of and in turn affected nineteenth-century law. Four of these are of special importance for the understanding of the legal thought of the last century and because of their bearing on the legal science of today: (1) the ethical idealistic interpretation and a special form thereof which may be called the religious interpretation; (2) the political interpretation; (3) positivist interpretations in terms of biology or ethnology, and (4) economic interpretations, whether idealistic or mechanical-positivist, or analytical-sociological[1]. Each of these sets up its own juristic god as the unchallengeable authority behind legal precepts and the ultimate causal agency in the development of law. But when these different forms have been looked into and we have examined them as to how far they give a satisfying account of legal phenomena in view of the demands of society of today and as to their effects when the ideas to which they gave rise were put into action in the administration of justice, we shall come to the conclusion that history as a juristic god has done no more for us than authority and philosophy which it succeeded.

---

[1] On history-writing and interpretation of history generally, see Barth, *Die Philosophie der Geschichte als Soziologie*, pp. 200–346 (2nd ed. pp. 483–809); Small, *General Sociology*, pp. 44–62; Cornford, *Thucydides Mythistoricus*; Fueter, *Geschichte der neueren Historiographie*; Gooch, *History and Historians in the Nineteenth Century*; Flint, *Historical Philosophy in France*; Croce, *Teoria e storia della storiografia*, 2nd ed., transl. as *On History* (1921); Croce, *Storia della storiografia Italiana nel secolo decimonono*. As to interpretations of jurisprudence and legal history, see Pound, "Political and Economic Interpretations of Legal History," *Proceedings American Political Science Assoc.* p. 95 (1912).

For the simple picture of the legal order painted by the historical school, with its one idea to which it attributed and by which it solved everything, must give way before the results of psychology and psychological sociology. We must give up the quest for the one solving idea. The actual legal order is not a simple rational thing. It is a complex, more or less irrational thing into which we struggle to put reason and in which, as fast as we have put some part of it in the order of reason, new irrationalities arise in the process of meeting new needs by trial and error.

On the one hand we must take account of the social or cultural needs of the time and place in all their possibilities of overlapping and of conflict and in all their phases, economic, political, religious and moral. On the other hand we must take account of suggestion, imitation, traditional faiths or beliefs, and particularly of the belief in logical necessity or authority expressing the social want or demand for general security. We must think not in terms of an organism, growing because of and by means of some inherent property, but once more, as in the eighteenth century, in terms of a building, built by men to satisfy human desires and continually repaired, restored, rebuilt and added to in order to meet expanding or changing desires or even changing fashions. We must think of a body of materials in actual use handed down from the past on which we work consciously and subconsciously to achieve the desires and satisfy the wants of the present; eking them out through suggestion and imitation, creating new ones now cautiously and now boldly when the old fail us, and moulding all to the form which those desires and wants have given to traditional faiths and beliefs; but held back by those traditional faiths and beliefs and especially in law by the rules and modes of thought of the art in which lawyers have been trained, become an instinct to follow logical compulsion and authority. Some such complex picture as this is given us by psychology and sociology in place of the simple pictures of the past. And yet in that complex picture there is something of each of those simple pictures to justify our looking at each of them in detail.

II

ETHICAL AND RELIGIOUS INTERPRETATIONS

In the ethical idealistic interpretation the idea which is realizing, which is unfolding in legal history, is an ethical idea—the idea of right[1]. On the one hand the jurist finds the idea and becomes able to grasp its content through history. On the other hand, when it is found, he proceeds to give it logical development. Thus there are two sides to the science of law, the historical and the logical. The combination gives a complete juristic method[2]. Later the historical and the metaphysical schools came to an understanding conceiving that the latter demonstrated the idea found by history, so that the two differed only in the side of the complete historico-metaphysical science of law to which chief attention was devoted[3]. But the metaphysical reinforcement did not seem necessary to English and Americans, who

---

[1] "Right receives a development in space and time. It has a history because it is practically realized by man. 'There is an unfolding of its nature in which it maintains its identity under change.'" Hastie, *Outlines of Jurisprudence*, p. 152 (1887). But this is translated from Friedländer (1847).

"A positive law, in its widest sense, may be defined as the expression of the idea of right involved in the relation of two or more human beings." Miller, *Lectures on the Philosophy of Law*, p. 9 (1884).

[2] See, for example, Hastie, *Outlines of Jurisprudence*, p. 153.

Compare also: "The object of the science of law is the principles of all the legal precepts which it is possible to promulgate by external law making." Kant, *Metaphysische Anfangsgründe der Rechtslehre*, Introduction, § A (1797).

"Philosophy of law or natural law is the science which deduces the highest principle or idea of right and law from the nature and destiny of man and of human society and develops it into a system of principles of right for all the fields of private and public law." Ahrens, *Naturrecht oder Philosophie des Rechts*, 1, § 1 (1870).

"The special science which we may properly call the philosophy of law... [is] the development of the idea of absolute justice which rests in every human mind and its application to the diverse relations which man may maintain about him." Boistel, *Cours de philosophie de droit*, 1, 3 (1899).

[3] "It is at once a philosophy, a science and an art. As a philosophy, its desire is to understand justice; as a science, its purpose is to explain the evolution of justice; as an art, its aim is to formulate those rules of conduct essential to the realization of justice." Adams, *Economics and Jurisprudence*, p. 8 (1897). See Geyer, *Geschichte und System der Rechtsphilosophie*, § 2 (1863); Prins, *La philosophie du droit et l'école historique* (1882).

were apt to speak of it slightingly[1]. Nevertheless the meta-physical element was decisive in the doctrine of the historical school. For the idea which it found was the idea of right held by and as formulated by the metaphysical jurists. In fact the historical method in jurisprudence was a historical verification of that idea.

Speaking generally, the conception of law and interpretation of legal history in terms of an ethical idea divided the allegiance of jurists with the political interpretation until the last quarter of the nineteenth century when new rivals arose. Usually the ethical interpretation was adhered to by those who followed the metaphysical or nineteenth-century philosophical school, while the political interpretation was adopted by professed adherents of the historical school. But there were many exceptions, for the two forms of idealistic interpretation were easily reconciled as modes of looking at or stating the same fundamental idea. Justification for treating them separately is to be found in the clearness with which they are distinguishable in typical examples and such treatment is convenient because the ethical interpreta-tion came first and as it were set the model for all subsequent nineteenth-century interpretations while the political interpreta-tion had an independent development in England and became an important factor in American decisions in constitutional law.

Closely related to the ethical interpretation is a special form of idealistic interpretation which conceives of the idea of right in terms of religion rather than of ethics and thinks of legal history as that part of the realization of a religious idea which has to do with its manifestation in right and law. Stahl argued in 1829 that a religion and a philosophical system alike was an endeavour to apprehend things in their total coherence according to their highest cause and purpose; that the Christian religion was such an apprehension of things and hence that law and the state were to be understood in terms thereof[2]. Stahl's execution of his design for a religious interpretation of law does not differ

---

[1] Pollock, *Essays in Jurisprudence and Ethics*, p. 28 (1882); Bryce, *Studies in History and Jurisprudence* (American ed.), p. 611 (1901); Gray, *Nature and Sources of the Law*, §§ 7-9 (1909).

[2] "The apprehension of things in their grand total coherence, according to their highest cause and purpose, we call world view. Every philosophical

in effect from the ethical interpretation of the metaphysical school to which he belonged. No one has sought to write a universal legal history from this standpoint, and religious interpretation of special periods of legal history, as, for instance, of classical Roman law in terms of the Stoic philosophy[1] and of the later Roman law in terms of Christianity, have found few adherents. The prevailing view has been that, after the stage of primitive law is passed, religion has played relatively a small part in legal history. Recently Riccobono has revived the question of the influence of Christianity upon Roman law after the fourth century[2]. English and American writers have not urged this interpretation and as such it has had no influence upon our actual law. Yet I venture to think that the influence of religious ideas in the formative period of American law was often decisive and that without taking account of Puritanism we shall fail to get an adequate picture of American legal history and shall not understand American law as it was in the last century[3]. I suspect also that some day we shall count religious ideas as no mean factor in the making of what are now the doctrines of English equity[4]. Undoubtedly such ideas played

system is such a world view. Every religion includes such a world view none the less, if with less thorough development. This is true also of the Christian religion. Now it is the latter which we take as the foundation of law and of the state." *Philosophie des Rechts*, II, 4 (1829).

[1] See Laferrière, *De l'influence du stoïcisme sur la doctrine des jurisconsultes romains* (1860); Hildenbrand, *Geschichte und System der Rechts- und Staatsphilosophie*, I, §§ 141–142 (1860); Pernice, *Labeo*, I, 16–17 (1873); Sokolowski, *Philosophie im Privatrecht*, §§ 2, 4–8, 11, 12, 30 (1902). On religious influence on law, see Coulanges, *La cité antique*, chaps. 1–4 (1864); Felix, *Der Einfluss der Religion auf die Entwickelung des Eigenthums* (1889); Bryce, *Studies in History and Jurisprudence*, Essay 13 (1901).

[2] *L' Influenza del cristianesimo nella codificazione di Giustiniano* (1909); "Cristianesimo e diritto privato," *Revista di diritto civile*, III, 37 (1911); "Communio e comproprietà," in Vinogradoff, *Essays in Legal History*, 33 (1913). See Troplong, *De l'influence du christianisme sur le droit civil des romains* (1843); Maas, *Der Einfluss der Christenthum auf das Recht* (1886); Baviera, "Concetto e limiti dell' influenza del cristianesimo sul diritto privato," *Mélanges Girard*, I, 67 (1912); de Zulueta, "The Girard Testimonial Essays," 30 *Law Quarterly Review*, 214, 216–217 (1914).

[3] I have considered this at length in *The Spirit of the Common Law*, Lecture II, "Puritanism and the Law," pp. 32–59 (1921); and in "Puritanism and the Common Law," *Proceedings Kansas State Bar Assoc.* 1910, 45, reprinted in 45 *American Law Review*, 811.

[4] I gave some examples in "Consideration in Equity," *Wigmore Celebration Essays*, p. 435.

a substantial part in the history of the modern Continental law of obligations[1]. So far as it directs attention to a factor which often may be of the first moment in shaping legal rules and doctrines and institutions the religious interpretation is by no means to be neglected.

It is not difficult to see why the first interpretation in point of time was ethical. The historical school succeeded to the leadership of the juristic world on the breakdown of the law-of-nature school. Its founder and its first adherents had been trained in the ideas of the latter. As Bekker puts it: "Savigny was...brought up in the enemy's camp [and]...had his first juristic training under the dominance of the very doctrine in opposing and rejecting which...lay his chief service. He was never wholly able to efface the stamp of this first impression[2]." His way of thinking was a reaction from the natural-law identification of the legal with the moral. According to the doctrine of his school law and morals had a common origin but diverged in their development so that his successors were able to throw over ethics and to hold that morals and what ought to be were matters with which the jurist had no concern[3]. But it was not easy to shake off the long-established connection which, indeed, was strengthened by the ambiguity of *ius* and its equivalents in the languages of Continental Europe, whereby one never can be wholly sure whether a writer is speaking of right or of law, in terms of ethics or in terms of jurisprudence, or of both—nor is the Continental jurist always careful to distinguish in his own thought. Thus analyses of law were likely to be also analyses of the idea of right; and after the period of growth from the sixteenth to the eighteenth century, with large infusions into legal systems from without, as for example in the case of the law merchant, a chief need was organizing, systematizing and harmonizing of the internal content of

[1] Salvioli, *Storia del diritto Italiano*, 8th ed. §§ 622–624. Compare also the influence of the church upon Continental criminal law, *id.* § 728.

[2] *Recht des Besitzes*, p. 3 (1880).

[3] "Investigation of the principles on which the direct improvement of substantive legal rules should be conducted belongs nevertheless not to the theorist on jurisprudence but to the theorist on legislation." Maine, *Early History of Institutions*, Lecture XII (1874). Cf. Clark, *Roman Private Law: Jurisprudence*, I, § 3 (1914).

bodies of law, in which analysis was the most effective
instrument. This need determined the first course of the
historical school.

System of the Roman law, carried into every detail whereby
every rule and doctrine is consistent internally and is made
part of a consistent whole, is one of the great practical achievements of nineteenth-century science of law. It gave us a
picture of an ideal legal system with reference to which jurists
in all lands could seek to put at least some corner of their legal
world in the order of reason. Its fruits may be seen in things as
far apart as English analytical jurisprudence—for Austin's debt
to the Pandectists of his day is obvious and Holland used the
later Pandectists avowedly and to excellent purpose—and the
German, Japanese, Swiss and Brazilian codes. The Romanists
who did this work were adherents of the historical school. They
did it by going back to the Roman texts after a period in which
jurists had relied on natural reason to tell them what law ought
to be and therefore must be. But their study of the texts was
for a special purpose directly connected with the law of their
own day. Accordingly they turned their energies to testing and
verifying the concepts reached by analysis of modern law by
analyzing the law of the past in terms thereof and so demonstrated that the systematic notions required for the ordering of
our law expressed the idea which was unfolding in the development of the rule or doctrine or institution in question. The rule
or doctrine or institution of today was the culmination of a
course of history[1] in which that systematic notion might be
traced from its embryo in the beginnings of Roman law or in
the oldest Germanic law, or according to later ideas, in an

[1] "The results of this inquiry as to the state of modern law [as to posses-
sion] are as follows: In modern times no doubt rules have been adopted which
were unknown to the Roman law. But the whole Roman theory is so far
from being infringed by those rules that on the contrary they may not be
understood except by treating them as further examples of that theory, the
validity of which is thus clearly recognized." Savigny, *Recht des Besitzes*,
§ 54 (1803).
But this "Roman theory" is a nineteenth-century generalization from the
Roman possessory interdicts and doctrines as to usucapion for the purposes
of modern problems. Later in the century Romanists modified it much
and still later, after Jhering, it was widely rejected. See Buckland, *Text Book
of Roman Law*, pp. 199–201.

Aryan *Urrecht*[1], to its full bloom in the maturity of law in the nineteenth century. The ethical interpretation was an incident —one might say a by-product—of this method whereby the Romanists of the historical school gave themselves a rational account of what they were doing. They were studying the law of the present as a stage in the history of Roman law and were studying the history of Roman law as a part of universal legal history.

In the latter respect, the ethical interpretation is related to the contemporary conception of universal history which obtained for a time in history-writing. There could be no writing of "universal history" unless there was a principle by which to select, reject and present the materials, and that principle was more likely to grow out of the present-day situation which the author sought consciously or subconsciously to explain to himself than to spring after the event from an unbiassed review of materials gathered without prepossession and studied without reference to a thesis. Writing of "universal history" within the compass of a single book required selection of a few facts, taken to be the significant or important facts, as if there could be an absolute significance or importance, which were then taken to demonstrate the principle with reference to which they had been chosen. So with the older sketches of universal legal history. In effect they were written from the standpoint of an ideal system of the modern Roman law and so succeeded in finding the germs of the analytical conceptions of that system in ancient legal institutions and in tracing the development of modern institutions therefrom along historical lines. Roman legal history was written by this method so well and in such detail with reference to every item of the modern law that it is giving us much trouble to distinguish the actual law of the first and second centuries from the juristic ideal picture of it which the historical school in the nineteenth century set up for us in its place. To a less extent the same thing happened in our

[1] Fustel de Coulanges, *La cité antique* (1864); Maine, *Early History of Institutions* (1874); Hearn, *The Aryan Household*, an Introduction to Comparative Jurisprudence (1878); Leist, *Altarisches Jus Gentium* (1889); Leist, *Altarisches Jus Civile* (1892–1896); Jhering, *Vorgeschichte der Indoeuropäer* (1894).

law. Doctrinal histories of this or that legal conception or legal precept were worked out, sometimes by courts but more often by text-writers or teachers, in which an analysis of the law of the nineteenth century was traced back into the Year Books and a principle was found latent in some meagrely reported, ambiguous and fragmentary pronouncement of a medieval court which had culminated in the latest decisions of English and American courts[1]. Thus the historical theory responded to the need of system, not merely in the law as a whole but in each department and branch and subdivision, which was felt both in Roman-law countries and in our own at the beginning of the last century.

To the foregoing reasons for the rise of the ethical interpretation we must add that Kant, who had been the chief agent in destroying the philosophical foundations of the eighteenth-century law of nature, had provided a metaphysical formula of right which was at hand to be made into a theory of law. Just as the Roman lawyers gave a legal content to the Greek philosophical conception of the just-by-nature and made it into natural law, Savigny put Kant's definition of right in terms of ordering the activities of free beings, co-existing in a condition of free contact with each other, by means of rules determining the boundaries within which each might securely exercise his freedom, and gave us a theory of law[2].

---

[1] Often these doctrinal histories had great systematic value and they played an important rôle in the systematizing of the different special departments of Anglo-American private law which went on so effectively in American law schools in the last quarter of the nineteenth century. Most of the "case books" prepared for use in those schools in the last two decades of the century proceed more or less in this way.

[2] "Acts of will or voluntary choice are thus regarded only in so far as they are free, and as to whether the action of one can harmonize with the freedom of another according to a universal law.

"Right, therefore, comprehends the whole of the conditions under which the voluntary actions of any one person can be harmonized in reality with the voluntary actions of every other person, according to a universal law of freedom.

"Every action is right which in itself, or in the maxim on which it proceeds, is such that it can co-exist along with the freedom of the will of each and all in action, according to a universal law." Kant, *Metaphysische Anfangsgründe der Rechtslehre*, Introduction, §§ A, B (1797).

Compare: "Man stands in the midst of the external world, and the most

Kant's formula of justice was the idea of right which was un-folding or realizing in legal history and every legal rule and doctrine and institution was a more or less complete or perfect expression of this idea. Moreover its future development could only be in the direction of more complete and perfect realiza-tion thereof. Down to the advent of the economic interpretation all idealistic and all positivist interpretations in one way or another came to this result[1]. For throughout the century social and legal philosophy were concerned to "reconcile government and liberty," and were troubled by the antithesis of a system of ordering men through an administrative organization or by the enforcement of legal precepts and of individual freedom resting on the autonomy of the human will. Administrative supervision of individual action and coercion by judicially enforced legal precepts were obvious facts called for by the demand for general security. Individual freedom of self-assertion was an ideal whose realization men were anxious that this supervision and coercion should advance or at least should not hinder. Kant's formula of right is an attempt at an absolute and universal solution of the difficulty. Indeed it seems to be the final form of an ideal of the social order which governed from the six-teenth to the nineteenth century; an ideal of the maximum of individual self-assertion as the end for which the legal order exists. The significance for jurisprudence of this problem of legal control and individual freedom and of Kant's solution thereof lies in this, that legal reasoning is the chief instrument by which compromise between the need of stability and the need of change is effected in the everyday administration of justice—by which, that is, new needs are met by means of old

important element in his environment is contact with those who are like him in their nature and destiny. If free beings are to co-exist in such a condition of contact, furthering rather than hindering each other in their development, invisible boundaries must be recognized within which the existence and activity of each individual gains a secure free opportunity. The rules whereby such boundaries are determined and through them this free opportunity is secured are the law." Savigny, *System des heutigen römischen Rechts*, I, § 52 (1840).

[1] I have discussed this more fully in a paper entitled, "The Philosophy of Law in America," *Archiv für Rechts- und Wirthschaftsphilosophie*, VII, 213, 385. Also in *The Spirit of the Common Law*, Lecture VI, "The Philosophy of Law in the Nineteenth Century," pp. 187 ff.

rules and institutions and adaptation to changing conditions is brought about with a minimum of outward infringement or warping of established precepts. But this legal reasoning is a process of analogical development by extension or restriction or generalization of precepts chosen and shaped with reference to an ideal of the end of the legal order. Thus a formulation of this end which is accepted generally by jurists in any time or place becomes a factor of no less importance in determining the course to be taken by the administration of justice for the time being than the mass of historically-given legal precepts which are consciously or unconsciously made over in its image.

Three such ideals of the end of law have governed at different times[1]. In the beginnings of the Roman law and in Germanic law there was a simple ideal of keeping the peace, of satisfaction of the social demand for general security put in its lowest terms. In Greek political philosophy, in the classical period and in the maturity of Roman law this ideal was replaced by one of maintenance of the general security mediately through the security of social institutions or, in other words, of satisfaction of the social interest in the security of social institutions. With the reception of the law of Justinian and of the philosophy of Aristotle in the later Middle Ages this orderly maintenance of the social *status quo* came to be the ideal of that period also. In the transition from a kin-organized society to a politically organized society on the model of kin-organization it was easy to pass from the idea of keeping the peace between kin-organizations to that of keeping everyone in his place in the social order of the city-state and of preventing friction with his fellow citizens through maintaining the social institutions that determined what this place was and the claims and duties which it involved. Greek philosophers sought to idealize this social order by ridding it of the remains of the older tribal or clan-organized society, thinking of men as put by law in the places for which their "nature" destined them or their "worth"

---

[1] I have discussed this subject at large in two papers, "The End of Law as developed in Juristic Thought," 27 *Harvard Law Review*, 605; 30 *Harvard Law Review*, 201.

suited them, and then held in that place by the legal order[1]. Roman lawyers gave the Greek theory practical effect by picturing social institutions which realized the nature of society— i.e. conformed to the ideal thereof—and legal institutions which realized the nature of law—i.e. conformed to an ideal of maintaining the pictured social order[2]. The Middle Ages took this over for a society organized on the basis of relations and thought of the end of law as maintenance of the social *status quo* by enforcing reciprocal claims and duties involved in relations established by tradition and maintained by authority[3].

Securing of a maximum of individual self-assertion, the third ideal of the end of law, begins to affect juristic thought in the sixteenth century, takes form in the seventeenth century and is developed fully in the metaphysical and historical jurisprudence of the nineteenth century. Its connection with the needs or desires of an era of discovery and colonization and trade, and later with the needs of an era of industrial development and expansion, is obvious. Men were no longer solicitous to maintain the social institutions by which effect was given to the system of reciprocal claims and duties of the parties to relations. They desired to be free of relations and duties that they might take advantage of the new opportunities afforded to the active and daring. The need was to satisfy the demands of individuals to assert themselves freely in the new fields of activity which were opening on every hand, and a new picture of the social order and of the end of law was painted in terms of this need. Beginning as a political theory of securing men in a natural (i.e. ideal) equality, it became a juristic theory of securing them in their natural rights (i.e. ideal qualities whereby it was just that they have certain things or do certain things), and by a further simplification became a theory of securing them in an abstract freedom of will. The first is a scholastic version proceeding upon the idea

[1] Plato, *Republic*, III, 397–398, *Laws*, VIII, 846d; Aristotle, *Nicomachean Ethics*, Bk V and Bk VII, 7, and 2–4, *Politics*, Bk I, 1, 9 and 13, Bk III, 1 and 4–5, Bk IV, 12. Compare St Paul in Ephesians v. 22 ff. and vi. 1–5.
[2] Cicero, *De Officiis*, II, 12, *De Republica*, I, 32; *Institutes of Justinian*, I, 1, pr. and § 3; Savigny, *System des heutigen römischen Rechts*, I, 407–410.
[3] Thomas Aquinas, *Summa Theologiae*, 1, 2, qu. 90–97; II, 2, qu. 57–80, 120, 122.

of the individual as the moral unit and hence as the political unit, replacing the idea of relation, and of the equal moral claims and moral responsibilities of these units[1]. The second is the natural-law version, proceeding on the idea of man as a rational entity and of the qualities of such an entity whereby he may co-exist with his fellows in a state of nature—i.e. in a condition in which those abstract qualities of a reasonable being are given their full effect[2]. The third is the metaphysical version of the nineteenth century. It begins with the individual consciousness as the ultimate datum and conceives of the problem of the legal order as one of reconciling conflicting free wills of conscious individuals independently exerting their wills in the different activities of life[3]. Kant formulated a theory of right in these terms as a reconciliation through universal rules whereby the will of each actor may co-exist with the wills of all others in action. As has been said, Savigny turned this into a theory of law and his successors interpreted jurisprudence and legal history in the light thereof.

We can make no greater mistake than to suppose that the speculations of the metaphysical jurists were without practical effect upon the law. We should be put on our guard, if by

[1] Franciscus de Victoria, *Relectiones theologicae*, I, 354, 375 (1557); Soto, *De justitia et jure*, I, qu. 5, art. 2; III, qu. 3, art. 2 (1589); Suarez, *De legibus ac deo legislatore*, I, 8, §§ 1, 2; I, 9, § 2; II, 19, § 9; III, 9, § 4; III, 11; III, 35, § 8 (1619).
[2] Grotius, *De jure belli et pacis*, I, 1, 3–6, 8–11; II, 1, 1; II, 1, 11; II, 10, 1; II, 17, 2, § 1 (1625); Pufendorf, *De jure naturae et gentium*, I, chap. 7, §§ 6–17; IV, chap. 4 (1672); Rutherforth, *Institutes of Natural Law*, I, 2, § 3 (1754).
[3] "I must in all cases recognize the free being outside of me as such, that is, must limit my liberty by the possibility of his liberty." Fichte, *Grundlage des Naturrechts*, I, 89 (1796).
"We may define right as a principle...governing the exercise of liberty in the relations of human life." Ahrens, *Cours du droit naturel* (8th ed.), I, 107 (1892).
"The fundamental axiom, which forms the basis of the whole system of natural justice I conceive to be, that one human being has no right to control for his own benefit the volition of another." Philipps, *Jurisprudence*, pp. 80–81 (1863).
"Law...has its basis in this, that men are beings endowed with a disposition to free exertion of will." Arndts' *Juristische Encyklopädie*, § 12 (1893).
"Hence that which we have to express in a precise way is the liberty of each limited only by the like liberties of all. This we do by saying: Every man is free to do that which he wills provided he infringes not the equal liberty of any other man." Spencer, *Justice*, § 27 (1891).

nothing else, by the wealth of literature from this standpoint in the first three quarters of the last century. When a popular exposition thereof, such as Ahrens' *Cours de droit naturel* could go through twenty-four editions in seven languages between 1837 and 1892, men must have been finding satisfaction in the metaphysical theory of law in more lands than one. I concede that the opinion that these speculations were wholly in the air and were without result has been wide-spread and has been advanced by writers of authority. Lord Bryce, for instance, speaks of nineteenth-century metaphysical jurisprudence almost with contempt, suggests that we should not expect much from "a metaphysician who thinks he understands law," and says that unless philosophical jurisprudence can help teach us the law that is, it is of little value[1]. But the law that is, in the sense of the nineteenth-century analytical jurist, is an illusion. It too is an ideal picture. Representing to himself the whole body of legal precepts as something made at one stroke on a logical plan to which it conforms in every detail, he conceives that he can discover this plan by analysis and he sets up a plan which explains as much as possible of the actual phenomena of the administration of justice and criticizes the unexplained remainder for logical inconsistency therewith. This is one way of insuring stability and giving orderly direction to change and has played an important rôle in legal science. But the confident dogmatism with which the analytical jurists condemn all painting of ideal pictures by others, assume that their picture is "the law," and conceive that they have demolished the claims of all other portrait painters by asserting that the jurisprudence of the latter is only "deontological"—dealing not with what is but with what ought to be—is but one more proof of the unhappy results of the water-tight-compartment learning of the nineteenth century. One need not say that the analytical jurists are lawyers pure and simple. Hence their picture has the merit of having in it nothing but law. But for that very reason it is

[1] *Studies in History and Jurisprudence*, 176–178, 191–192, 203–204, American edition, 611–612, 631–634. See also his remarks before the Association of American Law Schools in 1907, 31 *Rep. Amer. Bar Assoc.* 1061, 1063.

less a picture of the law than any of the others. For the thing
pictured is not something that patiently sits for a portrait. It
is continually shifting and while the analytical portrait is painting
it becomes an ideal picture of something past. The logical plan
of the analytical jurist may be used to give direction to the
minor shiftings. But the major shiftings that make the law what
it is in any time and place are given direction by ideas from
without the law, and it is with these that the metaphysical
jurists had to do. Metaphysical jurisprudence gave the historical
school its idea of right and hence fixed the lines of its ethical
interpretation of legal history. In other words the historical
critique to which legal rules and doctrines and institutions were
subjected in the last century comes directly from these meta-
physicians who thought they understood law. It is not the
work of lawyers nor of historians. It came from Kant and
Hegel.

Through the historical school the doctrines of metaphysical
jurisprudence affected profoundly the actual course of decision
and of legal writing. They gave the design which the historian
verified out of legal history; they drew the picture by which
judge and jurist shaped the materials of the past in making the
law of the present. For example, the arguments of the late
James C. Carter were no small factor in fashioning American
judicial decisions of the last quarter of the nineteenth century
and his posthumous book has in a measure kept his influence
alive. But his ideas were those of the metaphysical historical
jurisprudence[1] which had been taught him in its first form by

[1] "But there is a guide which, when kept clearly and constantly in view,
sufficiently informs us what we should aim to do by legislation and what
should be left to other agencies. This is what I have so often insisted upon
as the sole function both of law and legislation, namely, to secure to each
individual the utmost liberty which he can enjoy consistently with the
preservation of the like liberty of all others. Liberty, the first of blessings,
the aspiration of every human soul, is the supreme object. Every abridgment of it demands an excuse and the only good excuse is the necessity of
preserving it. Whatever tends to preserve this is right, all else is wrong."
Law; Its Origin, Growth and Function, 336–338 (1907). This shows the
influence of the second generation of the historical school and of the positivists.
In earlier writings he thought in terms of Savigny's theory of law and of the
ethical interpretation. Thus: "That the judge cannot make the law is accepted from the start. That there is already existing a rule by which the case
must be determined is not doubted....It is agreed that the true rule must

a student of Savigny when Mr Carter was himself a student[1]. Again, the influence of the Pandectists of the historical school on the English analytical jurists has been remarked. One of the main achievements of the Pandectists is the theory of the legal transaction, of the declared will to which the law gives effect, thereby realizing the freedom of the declarant by making his will operative in the external world. This theory in its dogmatic legal form was taken over by English writers on contracts, who persistently sought to shape the English law of contracts thereto and more than once succeeded in inducing the courts to adopt their conception. Again, note the attempt in the nineteenth century to restate the common law of public callings in terms of the modern Roman-law theory of a legal giving effect to the will of contracting parties, and the more successful attempt to make over the Anglo-American law of torts by a modern Roman-law generalization of no liability without fault. This generalization was never adequate to explain all the phenomena of liability for tort in the common law. But the phenomena which were not consistent with it were pronounced "historical anomalies," and the metaphysical-analytical theory was taken to be the idea which had been realizing through the whole evolution of legal liability, reaching its most complete development in the modern law. Accordingly writers did not hesitate to predict the eventual disappearance of the doctrine of *Rylands* v. *Fletcher* from the law and even to suggest that

somehow be *found*. Judge and advocates, all together, engage in the *search*. Cases more or less nearly approaching the one in controversy are adduced. Analogies are referred to. The customs and habits of men are appealed to. Principles already settled as fundamental are invoked and run out to their consequences; and finally a rule is deduced which is declared to be the one which the existing law requires to be applied to the case. In this the things which are plain and palpable are, (1) that the whole process consists in a *search* to find a rule; (2) that the rule thus sought for is the *just* rule—that is, the rule most in accordance with the sense of justice of those engaged in the search; (3) that it is tacitly assumed that the sense of justice is the *same* in all those who are thus engaged—that is to say, that they have a common standard of justice from which they can argue with, and endeavour to persuade each other; (4) that the field of search is the habits, customs, business and manners of the people, and those previously declared rules which have sprung out of previous similar inquiries into habits, customs, business and manners." *The Ideal and the Actual in Law*, 10–11 (1890).

[1] See Cushing, *Introduction to the Study of Roman Law*, §§ 269–279 (1854). These lectures were delivered in 1849, as stated in the advertisement p. v.

the disappearance was going on under our eyes by means of judicial smothering of the doctrine with exceptions[1]. For a time these views of learned writers had a marked effect upon the course of decision in America. More recently there has been a revival of the doctrine in America to enable the law to meet new forms of menace to the general security. Also the English courts have refused to limit the doctrine to adjacent freeholders and have extended it to new situations of fact[2]. Moreover absolute liability of those who maintain dangerous animals and for trespassing animals, supposed to be disappearing anomalies, have shown unexpected vitality. The English Court of Appeal has upheld the former to the very verge in the case of an animal wrongfully turned loose by an intermeddler[3] and has applied the latter to collateral consequences of the trespass[4], distinguishing a nineteenth-century decision which seemed to require knowledge of the propensity or condition that led to the consequences[5]. Such things indicate, what we may verify on every side of the law today, that the reign of the historico-metaphysical thinking as to the end of law is past. But the wide-spread criticism of these decisions, the general feeling that they infringe principles of the common law, the extent to which the dogma of no liability without fault was translated into actual legal precepts in the last century, the decisions of American courts that workmen's compensation acts were unconstitutional because legislative imposition of liability without fault was not

---

[1] "In every case of the kind which has been reported since *Rylands* v. *Fletcher*, that is, during the last 25 years, there has been a manifest inclination to discover something in the facts which took the case out of the rule....There are some authorities which are followed and developed in the spirit, which become the starting point of new chapters of the law; there are others that are only followed in the letter, and become slowly but surely choked and crippled by exceptions." Pollock, *Law of Fraud in British India*, 53–54 (1894). Compare Salmond, *Torts*, 4th ed. 233, arguing that the doctrine has no application if no one has been negligent. Also, Thayer, "Liability Without Fault," 29 *Harvard Law Review*, 801.

[2] *Charing Cross Electricity Supply Co.* v. *Hydraulic Power Co.*, [1914] 3 K.B. 772, 779, 785; *Musgrove* v. *Pandolis*, [1919] 2 K.B. 43.

[3] *Baker* v. *Snell*, [1908] 2 K.B. 352, 355.

[4] *Theyer* v. *Purnell*, [1918] 2 K.B. 333. Compare "The doctrine is a stubborn archaism," Pollock, *Torts*, 11th ed. 501, note *y*.

[5] *Cox* v. *Burbidge*, 13 C.B., N.S., 430 (1863). See Pollock, *Torts*, 11th ed. 500.

due process of law[1], and the pronouncement of no less an authority than Judge Baldwin that the fellow-servant rule expressed an idea of right and hence that Congress could not compel a state court to disregard it in a cause within the purview of federal legislative power[2]—such things are ample proof that the speculations of the metaphysical school were indeed practical in the sense that they were effective agencies in bringing about practical results.

With the second generation of the historical school the ethical interpretation was superseded by or passed into the political interpretation. Some of its defects passed over into the new doctrine and may be considered more conveniently in that connection. At this point it is enough to suggest five reasons for the failure of the ethical interpretation to satisfy the demands made upon the science of law by the conditions of the end of the nineteenth century and of the present. These reasons are: (1) the fallacy of continuity of the content of legal conceptions, (2) the over-rigid tying down of the process of trial and error by projecting an analysis of the law of one time back into history and then making it a measure of legal development for all time, (3) the tendency to fill the abstract content of the idea of right according to the personal feelings, training or associations of judge or jurist so that instead of fortifying him against these things the ethical interpretation justified him in following them, (4) the tendency of its adherents to make ingenious justifications of doctrines rather than to criticize them, and (5) the romantic tendency characteristic of the time when the historical school arose.

One phase of the fallacy of continuity of content is to be seen in the tendency to a history of names, assuming the content to be constant because the name is constant. An example may be seen in judicial application of the privileges-and-immunities clause of the American federal constitution to corporations doing business in states other than those under whose laws they were organized. When the clause was first applied to such a

---

[1] *Ives* v. *South Buffalo R. Co.*, 201 *New York Reports*, 271, 285–287, 293–295 (1911).
[2] *Hoxie* v. *New York R. Co.*, 82 *Connecticut Reports*, 352.

situation corporation meant a state-granted monopoly. Today in America it means a group of business adventurers doing business by means of a company with limited individual liability. But this changed content was lost sight of. The present meaning was projected back into the old interpretation and thus that interpretation was brought forward to meet a new situation. The resulting struggle between legal authority and the needs of commerce has produced a logically impossible condition in the decisions upon the position of the corporations of one state doing business in another. A process of meeting the needs of today by trial and error is going on, but it is hampered by the assumption of historical continuity[1].

A like phenomenon may be seen in history-writing generally in the last century. For example, Croce tells us that the neo-Ghibelline historians of modern Italy assumed that their concept of united Italy was the same as that of Macchiavelli, that their democratized and nationalized nineteenth-century ideal of an Italian people was the same as the sixteenth-century ideal of a concentration of political authority in a single sovereign prince; that their ideal born of an age which had overthrown the political regime which Macchiavelli admired was identical with his conception of critical politics arising from comparison of the political state of Italy with that of other countries of Europe. And he points out that this nineteenth-century ideal was not adapted to the writing of Italian history because from the Lombard invasion to the nineteenth century the unity which it assumed had not existed[2]. Speaking of interpretations of Italian history in terms of church and state, he says: " Church and state are not fixed entities which enter into relations and now one subverts the other, now they accord and now they turn indifferent shoulders to one another; and the history of these institutions cannot be written with the criterion of the state nor with that of the church nor with that of neutrality between state and church. According to the times the church is the state or the state is the true church[3]." The writing of

---

[1] See Henderson, *The Position of Foreign Corporations in American Constitutional Law* (1918).
[2] *Storia della storiografia Italiana nel secolo decimonono*, I, 181–182.
[3] *Id.* II, 188–189.

legal history is peculiarly liable to this sort of error because of the dogmatic fiction that the legal rule applied for the first time to a new case has existed from the beginning and the desire of the lawyer to rest all rules and all legal conceptions upon an incontestable basis in the unchangeable nature of things or in eternal unchangeable reason or in immemorial usage.

Another phase of the same fallacy may be seen in the idea of continuity of the content of legal systems, ignoring the successive infusions from without and from outside of the law and thinking that because there had been no definite tearing down of the whole at one time and no definite replacing of the whole at one stroke, but instead a long succession of crumblings, repairings, partial replacings, remodellings and additions, and because the more thorough of these were often called "restorations," the present structure was to be identified with the one which first stood upon the site. Thus in the ethical interpretation of Roman and Continental legal history there is the assumption that there was at work "a rational and scientific element expressing the constant needs of human nature and endowed with such flexibility that it was able to produce the Twelve Tables, the so-called middle jurisprudence, the perpetual edict of Hadrian, the Theodosian code, and finally the codification of Justinian; could serve as a powerful aid to the canon law; could live along with the feudal law and end by rooting it out in Western legislation; could resist the French Revolution which made war upon it when it had supported all the powers that the Revolution fought against, and finally could remain in the bosom of that people under the name of the civil code[1]." It was easy to write a like story of the continuity of the common law from Norman England to twentieth-century America, assuming the unfolding of an idea endowed with like flexibility and persistence and portraying a series of struggles, with the church in the twelfth century, with the movement for reception of the Roman law in the sixteenth century, with Tudor and Stuart kings in the sixteenth and seventeenth centuries, with post-Revolutionary hostility to things English in America at the end of the eighteenth and beginning of the nineteenth century and with popular

[1] Blanch, quoted by Croce, *id.* II, 21.

impatience of constitutional restraints in the era of popular legislation in America of today. But in each case how much of what we begin with do we end with? The historical school thought of each in terms of the growth of an organism, in terms of a development by the force of something working from within, wholly apart from human activity. Blackstone's analogy of an English castle made into a modern house, of something made over by men for their needs, by constant adaptations of and addings to the old materials, is quite as well taken. Indeed we might well compare these systems of law to one of the old churches in Rome. Perhaps the Servian wall is in its foundations and an old pre-Christian basilica was the first edifice. It was made over into a church in the fourth century. Perhaps in the ninth century a new church was built on the foundations and with part of the walls. It was rebuilt in the twelfth century and many stones and ornaments and some of the old mosaics and paintings were incorporated. It was restored frequently in later centuries and overhauled thoroughly in an eighteenth-century restoration in the baroque style of the time. The nineteenth century has added new chapels and monuments and has sought sometimes to bring to light some fragments of antiquity. How much of what men use today is the Servian wall or the Roman basilica, or the church in which the fifth-century council sat, or the church of the twelfth century or even the church of the Renaissance? Such a picture is much nearer the truth than the picture of organic evolution and continuous identity with which the historical school made us familiar.

Behind the fallacy of continuity of content is the metaphysical doctrine of the progressive unfolding of an idea. Put in action in legal thinking it makes an ideal of the law of one time and place a rigid measure for all law. And as ends or wants or desires of that time and place gave form to that ideal, the requirements of those ends become fixed as limits within which alone the requirements of the different ends of another time and place may be met. We shall see this phenomenon more marked in connection with the political interpretation. But I may cite as an example the will-theory of obligation in the modern Roman law and the attempts of text-writers and of courts following them to impose that theory upon our common law. Savigny was the leading exponent of that theory[1]. From him it passed into English and American treatises on the law of contracts[2] and has been taught as orthodox Anglo-American law by many who nevertheless professed to regard our law as a product of the spirit of our people.

What are abstract ideas in the hands of philosophers get a concrete content when they come into the hands of lawyers. This content is commonly derived from the modes of thought, rules of art and legal precepts in which the lawyer has been trained. This happened in the classical Roman law in which natural law got its content by idealization and generalization of the traditional modes of thought and rules of art of the jurisconsults and of the legal precepts which they had learned from their teachers. It happened conspicuously in the beginnings of American constitutional law when the natural rights of man got a legal content from the immemorial common-law rights of Englishmen as expounded by Coke and Blackstone[3]. But the ethical interpretation in terms of an idea of right tempted jurist and judge to fill out the content with something more than law or than law moulded with reference to the social order of the time and place. It seemed to justify him in finding in legal precepts a declaration or a realizing of what seemed to him personally to be right. Carried into action in American constitutional law, the result of this way of thinking has been, as Mr Justice Holmes puts it, "that in some courts new principles have been discovered outside the body of...[constitutions], which may be generalized into acceptance of the economic doctrines which prevailed about fifty years ago and the wholesale prohibition of what a tribunal of lawyers does not think about right[4]." If any one thinks this an overdrawn statement, I invite his attention to some examples that are not controversial. In one case, decided in Georgia during the Civil War, the

---

[1] *Das Obligationenrecht*, II, § 52 (1853).

[2] Anson, *Contracts*, pt. II, chaps. 2, 6; Pollock, *Contracts*, chap. 1, modified in later editions. See Williston, *Contracts*, 1, § 21.

[3] I have discussed this phenomenon in *The Spirit of the Common Law*, Lecture IV, "The Rights of Englishmen and the Rights of Man."

[4] "The Path of the Law," 10 *Harvard Law Rev.* 456, 467; *Collected Papers*, 184.

Supreme Court of the State, in passing on the validity of a Confederate conscription act, assumed as a matter of course that the doctrine of states' rights expressed the idea of right of which the Confederate constitution was declaratory and so laid down that legislation in derogation thereof was invalid, without reference to any particular constitutional limitations, as contrary to an absolute, unwritten, fundamental law[1]. In another case, decided in 1871, a state statute making desertion for two years a ground of divorce ran counter to the religious views of one of the judges of the highest court of the state, and he laid down dogmatically that the statute should not be enforced on the ground of conflict with fundamental law[2]. An interpretation of legal history and of law that leads to such results is by no means always a stabilizing force.

One of the merits of the historical school was that by studying the origin and development of legal precepts and doctrines it was able to expose the specious reasons invented after the event by eighteenth-century writers from the philosophical standpoint to explain and justify historical survivals which had ceased to serve useful ends in the administration of justice. But the arbitrariness of the schemes to which it was assumed all legal history and hence all future legal development must conform, led the historical jurists to give up criticism of legal precepts with reference to their effects in action or their adequacy to the ends of the legal order and to turn their learning to ingenious justification. Thus Savigny gives a highly artificial justification of the anomalous rule that in a legacy upon impossible or illegal condition precedent the condition shall be treated *pro non scripto*; a rule growing out of *favor testamenti* in republican Rome, when a will was a means of perpetuating a household, and quite out of place when applied to a modern will[3]. Thus also Dean Ames, conceiving that the historical distinction between law and equity expressed an idea and hence was fundamental and necessary, objected to direct relief by a common-law proceeding or in a common-law court, although in jurisdictions where legislation allowed complete relief in one pro-

---

[1] Jenkins, J., in *Jeffers* v. *Fair*, 33 *Georgia Reports*, 347, 365–366, 367 (1862).
[2] Turney, J., in *Lanier* v. *Lanier*, 5 *Heiskell* (*Tennessee Reports*), 462, 472 (1871).
[3] *System des heutigen römischen Rechts*, III, § 124.

ceeding, and argued for a round-about proceeding in equity, in the case of a creditor of a partnership who took a bond under seal made by an insolvent partner as the bond of all and so lost his claim against the solvent partners[1].

Others have remarked the connection between the modes of thought of the founders of the historical school in jurisprudence and the general Romantic movement of the time. The so-called historical epos of Romantic history-writing has its counterpart in the writing of legal history. The most notable of these historico-legal epics was the epos of Anglo-American public law, so popular a generation ago. It usually began with a sort of prologue picturing the self-governing local group of the Germanic peoples, the mark, the *gemot*, the Swiss *Landesgemeinde*, and the New-England town meeting[2]. The main action began with an interpretation of Magna Carta in terms of an eighteenth-century bill of rights and culminated in an interpretation of the contests between courts and crown in seventeenth-century England in terms of American constitutional law. Such things are entirely comparable to the epics of Italian history, inspired by the idea of a united and liberated Italy which Croce has dissected so acutely. The epos of Anglo-American public law was inspired no less clearly by the desire of American lawyers to find an unchallengeable foundation for the power of American courts with respect to unconstitutional legislation.

Yet there were elements of truth in the ethical interpretation and this phase of historical jurisprudence achieved something for the science of law. There was a sound instinct behind it in that it sought to give a picture of the end of law and such pictures are the guide by which jurists find a way to make the law adequate to satisfying the wants of society through adapting its precepts and doctrines and institutions to new and changed demands. Also there was truth in its picture of continuity in that there is continuity in traditional modes of professional thought and in traditional rules of art and these modes of thought and rules of art are a powerful restraining force when

[1] *Cases on Equity Jurisdiction*, II, 280, note (1904).
[2] This was usually drawn from Freeman, *Growth of the English Constitution*, chap. I (1872). See also Adams, *The Germanic Origin of New England Towns*, I, 245 (1882).

the materials of a legal system are reshaping and applying to new uses to meet new wants or new forms of old wants. The religious interpretation rendered an important service in turning our attention to the real nature and origin of many phenomena in Anglo-American common law and in American legislation which must be attributed in largest part to Puritan influence. Above all, however, the ethical interpretation was of service in combatting the persistent tendency of nineteenth-century lawyers in England and in America, under the influence of analytical jurisprudence and of the dogma of separation of powers, to insist that lawyer and judge and jurist had nothing to do with ethics; that they were concerned only with a critique of law drawn from the law itself by analysis of its content[1]. In so doing it helped to counteract the tendency to what Sir William Erle called "strong decisions"—decisions, as he described them, "opposed to common sense and common convenience," but taken to be required by the exigencies of legal logic as applied to given legal premises[2]. In such decisions there was often pride in demonstrating that law was one thing and morals another and that a precept might be legally valid and yet morally unfortunate[3]. The doctrine that an ethical idea was unfolding in legal development and that legal precepts were manifestations or realizations of an idea of right was in its time a useful antidote to the notion that the words "be it enacted" or "it is considered and adjudged" were sufficient to justify anything that might follow.

[1] Pollock, *First Book of Jurisprudence*, pt. 1, chap. 2 (1896); Gray, *Nature and Sources of the Law*, §§ 642–657 (1909).

[2] "I have known judges, bred in the world of legal studies, who delighted in nothing so much as in a strong decision. Now a strong decision is a decision opposed to common sense and common convenience....A great part of the law made by judges consists of strong decisions, and as one strong decision is a precedent for another a little stronger, the law at last, on some matters, becomes such a nuisance that equity intervenes or an Act of Parliament must be passed to sweep the whole away." Sir William Erle, Chief Justice of the Common Pleas, 1859–1866, *ex rel.* Senior, *Conversations with Distinguished Persons* (1880 edition), 314.

[3] "The doctrine of tacking [incumbrances] has received judicial reprobation many times confirmed. But notwithstanding, in some of the cases where the doctrine has been applied...is it not possible perhaps to detect a note rather of triumph than of surrender—the triumph of art, not the surrender of justice to the binding force of unfortunate precedent." Willoughby, *The Distinctions and Anomalies Arising out of the Equitable Doctrine of the Legal Estate*, 71–72 (1912).

III

THE POLITICAL INTERPRETATION

OUR modern science of law begins in the thirteenth century as a branch or an application of theology, an attempt to support the authority of the academically taught Roman law by philosophical theology. It was emancipated from theology in the sixteenth century by the Protestant jurist-theologians, notably Hemmingsen, whom Grotius followed in this respect. In the seventeenth and eighteenth centuries it was united with politics and international law, a common philosophical foundation serving for each after which it was usual to expound successively the general principles of politics, the general principles of jurisprudence, and a system of the law of nations. In the nineteenth century international law became a subject of itself, jurisprudence and politics grew apart, and jurisprudence as a separate science developed three distinct methods. So far was this specialization carried that each method came to be thought of as self-sufficient and claimed to be a whole, if not the whole, science of law. As has been seen, the ethical interpretation kept up a certain connection with ethics, handed down from the exclusively philosophical legal science of the eighteenth century. But with the progress of the historical school this disappeared and the Hegelian contrasting of law and morals definitely superseded the tendency to identify them. On the other hand the rise of the political interpretation made a new connection between law and politics which has stood fast. For the present tendency is away from the extreme specialization and rigid setting off of narrowly defined sciences which was the fashion in the last century. Today we seek to unify all the social sciences and to treat jurisprudence merely as one of the group, holding that none is self-sufficient. Next to its functional attitude, this rejection of the conception of a wholly independent science of law, drawn exclusively from the law itself and ignoring every other department of knowledge as irrelevant to its problems and of no value for its ends, is the most significant feature of recent juristic thought. The narrowly limited legal science, indifferent to and even intolerant of light from without, characteristic of the nineteenth century, reached its high-water mark in the English and American analytical jurisprudence of the immediate followers of Austin. The political interpretation was the first of a succession of reactions therefrom which have given jurisprudence a new aspect in the twentieth century.

Philosophically the ethical interpretation represents the influence of Kant upon historical jurisprudence, resulting in an interpretation of legal history and hence of law in terms of Kant's theory of right. The political interpretation represents the influence of Hegel. It is an interpretation in terms of Hegel's proposition that right is "freedom as an idea." The word which we translate sometimes as "law" and sometimes as "right," which I have translated as "right" in the foregoing formula, does not mean either exactly nor may we understand it by combining the two. Hegel was formulating a conception of what I have been calling the end of law. He means that which the legal order is conceived as existing to bring about; what we mean by "justice" when we say that the law exists as a means to justice. Thus, he holds, law realizes the idea of freedom, the idea that "existence generalized is existence of the free will[1]." In the hands of jurists this interpretation regards the idea in its political aspect or, we may say, takes a political idea to be the idea which is realizing in legal history and is unfolding in legal rules and doctrines and institutions. Looked at legally and politically the idea is freedom or liberty. Ideal perfection in human relations is liberty. Jurisprudence and politics have to do with different but closely allied phases of liberty as realized in civil relations[2].

[1] "This is right: that existence generalized is existence of the free will. Accordingly generalized it is freedom as an idea." Hegel, *Grundlinien der Philosophie des Rechts*, 61 (1820).

[2] "The proximate object of jurisprudence, the object which it seeks as a separate science, is liberty. But liberty being the perfect relation between human beings, becomes a means towards the realization of their perfection as human beings. Hence jurisprudence, in realizing its special or proximate object, becomes a means towards the realization of the ultimate object which it has in common with ethics." Lorimer, *Institutes of Law*, 2nd ed.

If on one side this more concrete conception of the end of law as freedom is due to Hegel, on another side it is related to rejection of the eighteenth-century faith in reason. It is a feature of the reaction from natural law and distrust of the creative juristic spirit such as we see it, for example, in Lord Mansfield. Thus Puchta, after laying down that the fundamental conception of right and law is freedom, adds that "reason is not the principle of freedom" but is an "element in human nature antagonistic to freedom[1]." For, he explains, reason imposes itself on the will and dictates this course of action or that. Hence we may not say, as did the seventeenth and eighteenth centuries, that right and law are reason. In that sense they are a check on freedom and hence antagonistic to it. What he means is that if the principle of law is reason, we shall get a great deal of law dictated by reason as what it demands with respect to human relations and hence much curtailment of freedom; whereas our eyes should be on freedom, not on curtailments of it, and we should have no restrictions simply realizing reason and no restrictions at all beyond those which realize freedom by bringing about that the existence of each is existence of the free will and giving effect to freedom as an idea. To do these things we must grasp the idea of freedom as it unfolds in history instead of trying to arrive at a system of natural law on the basis of reason. This mode of thought was carried to its logical conclusion by the later generation of the historical school who became positivists. If, they argued, law is the science of liberty, every rule of law is an evil, since all regulation of liberty

354–355 (1880). Compare also the quotations in note 3, ante p. 32, and from Carter's *Law; Its Origin, Growth and Function*, in note 1, ante p. 34. It will be seen that these put more concretely the idea of the ethical interpretation.

[1] "Freedom is the foundation of right, which is the essential principle of all law. Hence we do not reach right as the principle of law by setting out from the notion of reason....For if the bad, as being evil, is the irrational, then freedom, which includes the possibility of evil, cannot be deduced from reason and *vice versa*. It would be much more in accordance with reason that the good should be realized of necessity. On the other hand it is contrary to mere reason that it comes through freedom, which does not exclude the possibility of evil. Thus reason is not the principle of freedom but is rather an element in human nature antagonistic to freedom; and it has shown itself to be such from the beginning." Puchta, *Cursus der Institutionen*, § 2 (1841).

is a limitation of it and right or the end of law is a maximum of
liberty. Thus it came to be said that law was a necessary evil;
evil because it restricted liberty and liberty was right, necessary
because without a certain minimum of restriction liberty was
not possible in the conflict and overlapping of human desires[1].
Without being carried consciously so far, the political interpretation was from the beginning a negative conception of the
function of jurist and legislator; it demanded a holding down of
the legal order to the necessary minimum—to the least which
was required to realize freedom in men's relations with each
other. The burden of proof was upon any one who proposed
a rule to show that it was clearly and imperatively required to
promote freedom. As it was put, coercion was to be reduced
to what was "absolutely necessary for the harmonious co-
existence of the individual with the whole[2]."

From the historical standpoint the political interpretation is
related to three movements in nineteenth-century writing of
history. In the beginning it was connected with the idea of
universal history. Hegel outlined a universal history of right in
his philosophy of right and law[3]. Puchta sketched a universal
legal history in the introduction to his institutional treatise on
Roman law, prefacing a history of Roman law which is a classic
of idealistic interpretation[4]. He showed us the idea of freedom
unfolding or realizing in a great chain of human experience—
Babylon, Egypt, Greece, Rome, Western Europe—with each

---

[1] "Law in the most general sense of the term is the science of liberty [5]."
"Every rule of law in itself is an evil, for it can only have for its object the
regulation of the exercise of rights, and to regulate the exercise of a right
is inevitably to limit it. On the other hand every rule of law which sanctions
a right, which preserves it from infringement, which protects it from a peril,
is good because in this way it responds to its legitimate end. Thus, if law
is an evil, it is a necessary evil." Beudant, *Le Droit individuel et l'état*,
5, 148 (1891).
Note that Beudant reaches this result by deduction from the metaphysical
theory, i.e. from the idea of liberty, or the free will of the conscious individual,
as Tom Paine reached it from the natural-law theory, i.e. from the idea of the
qualities of a reasonable creature in a state of nature, or as Spencer reached
it by observation of a "manifest tendency" throughout civilization to "extend
the liberties of the subject." Paine, *Rights of Man*, 46, 48, 50 ff. (1791);
Spencer, *First Principles*, § 2
[2] Lioy, *Philosophy of Right*, transl. by Hastie, I, 121.
[3] *Grundlinien der Philosophie des Rechts*, §§ 346–347 (1820).
[4] *Cursus der Institutionen*, § 9 (1841).

handing on its experience to the next in which the idea pro-
gressively rids itself more and more of the purely accidental
and unfolds more and more completely. Gans even wrote a
universal history of the law of inheritance from this standpoint[1].
It was indeed a remarkable feat. For it requires some logical
acrobatics to interpret collateral inheritance, transition from
the *favor testamenti* of republican Rome to the opposite doctrine
in the modern law, Roman restrictions on testamentary disposition, such as the *Lex Falcidia*, and their further development in modern law, and Justinian's 118th novel, with all the
changes which modern legislation has rung upon its scheme of
cognation, as realizations of an idea of freedom. Perhaps I ought
to say that this sort of legal historical romance, written to show
us the idea of freedom realizing itself in legal history, is quite
another thing from the universal legal history of Kohler and the
neo-Hegelians of today. Kohler would study the relation of
law to civilization in order to enable us to make the law of today
express the civilization of today and to make it further rather
than hinder civilization[2]. In other words there is an active
creative element in Kohler's universal legal history which is
characteristic of recent juristic thought.

A philological tendency, due to the effect of comparative
philology of the Indo-European languages, which gave an
impetus to comparative method in all directions, was manifest
also in the historical school of jurists. The attempt to reconstruct
the *Ursprache* suggested reconstruction of the Aryan *Urrecht*
and the place which Sanskrit held in philology suggested study
of the monuments of Hindu law and the possibility of finding
legal ideas in their simplest form in this body of primitive legal
institutions just as the roots of words were identified through
the study of Sanskrit. Thus a comparative Indo-European law
and politics was one of the forms taken by the political interpretation. But the tendency was to restrict study of legal history
to arbitrarily chosen periods which were assumed to be the

---

[1] *Das Erbrecht in weltgeschichtlicher Entwickelung* (1825). Only a part of
the projected work was written.
[2] "Rechtsphilosophie und Universalrechtsgeschichte," in Holtzendorff,
Enzyklopädie der Rechtswissenschaft, 1, 6th ed. 1904, 7th ed. 1913. Not in
prior editions.

significant periods in legal development[1]. For the most part legal history meant history of Roman law down to Justinian, history of Germanic law to the reception of Roman law, and history of English law from the twelfth to the fifteenth century.

It is noteworthy that the historical school had an instinctive dislike of the period from the end of the sixteenth to the end of the eighteenth century in which the law was remade under the influence of a creative philosophical theory and became the body of legal materials upon which the nineteenth-century systematists were at work. In the United States there came to be a cult of the Year Books and in England a tendency was manifest in judicial decision to appeal from the eighteenth century to the "old law of England" as shown in the medieval books. Thus in the law as to gifts of chattels, in which the idea of effectuating the declared intention of the donor had made headway steadily against the Germanic idea of seisin during the eighteenth century[2] and in spite of a decision of Lord Tenterden[3] had been asserted in a long line of judicial pronouncements in the nineteenth century[4], the Court of Appeal in 1890 conceived the question one to be determined entirely by reference to Bracton and the Year Books[5]. In this case the result was happy. But the method of determining whether to fasten the notion of seisin upon a modern legal transaction or to carry forward a movement of the law in the direction of giving effect more fully and freely to declared intention—the method of deciding such a question by resort to the medieval books, ignoring the growing period of the seventeenth and eighteenth centuries, was unhappy[6]. In England the reign of this method

[1] See some comments on this in Leonhard, "Methods Followed in Germany by the Historical School of Law," 7 *Columbia Law Rev.* 573, 577 (1907); Kantorowicz, *Zur Lehre vom richtigen Recht*, 8 (1909).
[2] Lord Hardwicke in *Ward* v. *Turner*, 2 Ves. Sr. 431, 442 (1752).
[3] *Irons* v. *Smallpiece*, 2 B. & Ald. 551 (1819).
[4] Parke, B., in *Ward* v. *Audland*, 16 M. & W. 870 (1847) and in *Ould* v. *Harrison*, 10 Exch. 572, 575 (1854); Crompton, J., in *Winter* v. *Winter*, 4 Law Times, N.S. 639, 640 (1861); Pollock, B., in *In re Harcourt*, 31 *Weekly Rep.* 578, 580 (1883); Cave, J., in *In re Ridgeway*, 15 Q.B.D. 447, 449 (1885). See Serjt. Manning's note *a*, 2 M. & G. 691 (1841).
[5] *Cochrane* v. *Moore*, 25 Q.B.D. 57.
[6] "It is revolting to have no better reason for a rule of law than that so it was laid down in the time of Henry IV. It is still more revolting if the

was relatively brief. In the United States it reigned longer and more autocratically and is only just disappearing from law teaching. For in America the philosophical and creative ideas of the eighteenth century persisted much longer than in England because the law-of-nature theory was the theory of our bills of rights and so was classical in our constitutional law and because the reception of the common law of England as the law of a pioneer society called for examination of every item with reference to its applicability to American institutions and conditions and hence for a certain creative attitude. The work of selection and reception was complete by the time of the Civil War, and the jurists of the last third of the century were in reaction from the ideas of the formative period of American common law, much as Savigny was in reaction from the juristic ideas of the end of the eighteenth century.

Legal history also might be vouched for the assertion that in nineteenth-century history-writing the "myth of the Middle Ages" was a new form of the state of nature[1]. The Middle Ages were idealized as a golden age in which modern legal and political institutions existed in their simple and natural forms. The writer of general history in this period disliked the time from the Reformation to the end of the eighteenth century because it was the time of development of centralized absolute governments and did not fit well with his conceptions of political and civil liberty which he considered he found manifested simply and imperfectly but unmistakably in the Middle Ages. So it was in law. On the Continent the historical jurist, if a Romanist, sought the simple original forms of our complex modern doctrines in the classical Roman law, or, if a Germanist, sought them in the Germanic law of the earlier Middle Ages. If an Englishman or an American he sought them in the Year Books. In this way each gave form to his distrust of the creative era in which rules were not suffered to develop spontaneously but were made over to accord with reason or rejected because

grounds upon which it was laid down have vanished long since and the rule simply persists from blind imitation of the past." Holmes, "The Path of the Law," 10 *Harvard Law Rev.* 457, 459, *Collected Papers*, 187.

[1] Compare Croce, *Storia della storiografia Italiana nel secolo decimonono*, I, 118–119.

4—2

not in accord therewith. As is not uncommon in such cases, the period of these phenomena, which did not accord with the dogma of the historian-jurist, was simply ignored as not significant.

Selection of periods for intensive historical study and disregard of other periods made the interpretation for which the historical school stood an artificial thing quite out of touch with the actual legal materials to which jurists sought to apply it. For, however much Coke may have misunderstood and misrepresented medieval English law, it was Coke's version thereof, not the actual fourteenth and fifteenth-century English law, that became the basis of the common law of America. No amount of historical criticism of Coke can alter that fact. No jurisdiction will change the foundations of its law because a historian shows that Coke had misunderstood the Year Books. So also it was Bartolus' version of Justinian that became the law of Continental Europe, not the law of Cicero or of the Antonines. It was wholly unhistorical to insist that agency should run forever along the clumsy contractual lines of the classical Roman law, and the contempt of the historical school for the *usus modernus* simply brought about an unhappy gulf between the law of academic teachers and the law of the courts which was to the disadvantage of each. Something of this sort threatened for a time in America when the historical school was at the height of its influence and teachers were disposed to find solutions of modern legal problems in oracular fragments in the Year Books.

Chiefly, however, the political interpretation was a part of the institutional movement in history-writing, of the rise of institutional history, of the idea that political institutions had a determining influence upon all things which was strong in the time of political ferment in the middle of the nineteenth century. For the moment the battles of the time were waging over institutions. On the Continent men sought to set up parliamentary institutions on the English model. In England the Reform Bill had opened the way for attacks upon all manner of institutions. The imperishable idea behind the institution, as distinguished from the accidents of which it was ridding itself in its historical development, became something of immediate practical importance. Croce says that scientific objectivity is more common in the histories of institutions such as histories of law[1]. To a layman, who must take his law from the very historical jurists whom he is criticizing, this may well seem true. It is by no means so clear when we look into the relation between institutional legal history and the wants and desires of the time in which it was written or of the group of men in which the historian found himself. We should expect that much might depend on the particular field in which the heated controversies of the time and place were waging—whether in religion or in politics or in social and economic beliefs. Histories of law may be affected easily in a time of transition and emergence of new class-consciousnesses, if the resulting struggle takes an economic turn and the nature and history of legal institutions come to be important for either side. Examples may be seen in the histories of the doctrine of judicial power over unconstitutional legislation and of the Supreme Court of the United States written during the agitation for recall of judicial decisions, advocated by Roosevelt, in the political campaign of 1912[2]. An analogous phenomenon may be seen also in the sympathy of jurists for Roman or for Germanic institutions and the stress they lay upon one or the other in their writing of institutional or of doctrinal legal history. One cannot doubt that somewhat exaggerated Germanic theories of a generation ago were connected with the rise of national consciousness in Germany nor that equally exaggerated attempts of some recent writers to find a Roman pedigree for everything in modern law are due to a newly excited race consciousness of Latin jurists. The writers of legal history may not flatter themselves that the nature of their subject in anywise exempts them from such innate difficulties in the telling of history.

Maine's famous generalization of legal history as a progress from status to contract[3] is the most important phase of the political interpretation both in its theoretic working out and in its practical consequences in the hands of courts and lawyers.

[1] *Id.* II, 35.
[2] Myers, *History of the Supreme Court of the United States,* is an extreme case.
[3] *Ancient Law,* chap. 5 (1861).

It is connected immediately with the institutional type of history and the movement in history-writing that gave rise thereto. Indeed one of Maine's chief writings is entitled "Early History of Institutions" and he studied legal institutions habitually rather than legal doctrines. His generalization of the progress from status to contract is the political interpretation put concretely in terms of legal institutions. It was universally accepted in Anglo-American juristic thought and governed down to the end of the century. It is still a force with which to reckon in American constitutional law.

At bottom Maine's theory is Hegelian. The idea which is realizing is liberty—free individual self-assertion. The way in which it is realizing is a progress from status to contract. It is a progress away from legal institutions and legal rules and legal doctrines in which one's legally recognized claims and legally enforced duties flow from a condition in which he is put or in which he finds himself without reference to his will and of which he cannot divest himself by any manifestation of his will. It is a progress toward legal institutions and rules and doctrines in which legally recognized claims flow from personality, from being a conscious free-willing human individual, and legally enforceable duties with respect to others are consequences of willed action, either in assuming the duties by some legally recognized form of undertaking or by willed culpable action or by willed action culpably carried on[1]. The gradual breakdown of status in the classical Roman law, the substitution of intent for form as a basis of liability, the conception of an intent implied in certain transactions and representing their nature or ideal

---

[1] "The movement of the progressive societies has been uniform in one respect. Through all its course it has been distinguished by the gradual dissolution of family dependency and the growth of individual obligation in its place. The individual is steadily substituted for the family as the unit of which civil laws take account. The advance has been accomplished at varying rates of celerity....But, whatever its pace, the change has not been subject to reaction or recoil....Nor is it difficult to see what is the tie between man and man which replaces by degrees those forms of reciprocity in rights and duties which have their origin in the family. It is contract. Starting, as from one terminus of history, in which all the relations of persons are summed up in the relations of family, we seem to have moved steadily towards a phase of social order in which all these relations arise from the agreement of individuals." *Ancient Law*, last paragraph but one of chap. 5.

content, the consequent development of a generalized law of contract in terms of pact or agreement clothed with certain forms as guarantees of a real intention so that the law might enforce them with assurance, the development of the modern law of delicts, following the French civil code, along the lines of Aquilian *culpa*—all these things make a strong case for this interpretation. But the proof from Roman law is in large part a proof from Roman law as interpreted by the first generation of the historical school in terms of Kant's formula of justice as an idea of right or as interpreted by the next generation in terms of an idea of freedom. In particular the idea of contract is Savigny's will-theory projected back into Roman law as an instrument for organizing the law of the nineteenth century. Moreover English legal history was not examined in making out the case, nor did the adherents of the political interpretation ever test it by an independent study of the common law. The theory came to common-law lawyers full blown and was assumed for our law without inquiry.

If we examine the evidence, we must ask at the outset whether Roman law shows anything more than a movement away from status; a progressive breaking down of legal institutions and rules and doctrines involved in an organization of society in households and a replacing of them by legal institutions and rules and doctrines called for by a politically organized society in which human beings were becoming the social and political and legal units. The remainder of the generalization is not drawn from the facts of Roman legal history but represents the juristic conception of the will as the central conception in jurisprudence, a metaphysical version of the idea that the end of law is to bring about a maximum of individual self-assertion. The conception of the legal transaction—*negotium, Rechts-geschäft, acte juridique*—is of the first importance for the system of nineteenth-century law. But this generalization was unknown to the Romans and it is at least disputable whether it represents Roman ideas of the basis of liability for undertakings. It is at least arguable that the Romans thought, not of giving effect to the will of the promisor, but of enforcing the duty of good faith involved in or arising from what he had done; that they proceeded on the Stoic conception of duty, not on the nineteenth-century conception of will[1]. What we have to interpret is a continual widening of the sphere of enforceable agreement. The historical school explained this phenomenon in terms of the problem of reconciling liability for undertakings and liability for civil wrongs with the widest possible abstract freedom. Hence they saw therein a continually widening and more complete giving effect to the will of the promisor. The Romans were not thinking in terms of any such problem. What they were thinking of was how to get rid of the old formal categories of liability and to enforce the reasonable expectations arising from the intercourse of men in a commercial society, in which security of transactions had become a social interest of the first magnitude, without disturbing the stability of the legal order. It had become a presupposition of the civilization of the time and place that those with whom one dealt in the general intercourse of society would act in good faith—would make good the expectations created by their conduct and would carry out their undertakings according to the expectations which the moral sentiment of the community attached thereto. The Romans used Stoic ideas of duty for this purpose as the nineteenth-century jurists used the metaphysical idea of will for the different purposes of their time. They were not striving to realize individual freedom as an idea. They were not giving effect to the will. Rather they were seeking to realize good faith and to give effect to moral duty[2]. But we may leave this question to the philosophical Romanist. At any rate, Maine's generalization, drawn exclusively from Roman legal history, will not fit the phenomena of the common law.

If we must find a fundamental idea in the common law, it is relation, not will. If the Romanist sees all problems in terms

[1] Erdmann, *History of Philosophy*, Hough's transl. I, 190; Zeller, *Stoics, Epicureans and Sceptics*, Reichel's transl. 265, 287. Compare the conception of τὸ καθῆκον as determined by reason with *naturalis obligatio*: *Dig.* 50, 17, 84, § 1; 12, 6, 38, § 2; 12, 6, 13, pr.; 12, 6, 64; 12, 6, 40, pr.; 4, 5, 2, § 2; 46, 1, 8, § 3.

[2] See the identification of law with morals in *Dig.* 1, 1, 1, § 1 and 1, 1, 11; *Inst.* 2, 7, 2; *Cod.* 8, 56, 1 and 10, and 4, 44, 2. Also texts as to good faith: Gaius, 2, § 43 and 4, §§ 61–62; *Dig.* 22, 1, 25, § 1; 41, 1, 40; 41, 1, 48, pr. and § 1; 41, 3, 4, § 20; 50, 17, 84, § 1; *Cod.* 3, 32, 22.

of the will of an actor and of the logical implications of what he has willed and done, the common-law lawyer sees almost all problems—all those, indeed, in which he was not led to adopt the Romanist's point of view in the last century—in terms of a relation and of the incidents in the way of reciprocal rights and duties involved in or required to give effect to that relation. Magna Carta, the foundation of our public law, is not an expression of the idea of individual freedom but a formulation of the rights and duties incident to the relation of the king and his tenants in chief[1]. Anglo-American public law, as a juristic and judicial development by treating new problems on analogies derived from Magna Carta, may be explained in terms of the reciprocal claims and duties of ruler and ruled, of government and governed, in a political relation, much more truly than in terms of contract or of giving effect to individual freedom by political institutions. But our private law is the field where the idea of relation is most conspicuous as a staple juristic conception. On every side we think not of transactions but of relations. We say law of landlord and tenant, not of the contract of letting. We say master and servant, not *locatio operarum*. We say law of husband and wife or of parent and child or of guardian and ward, or for the whole, law of domestic relations, not family law. We say principal and agent, not contract of mandate; principal and surety, not contract of suretyship; vendor and purchaser, not contract of sale of land. We think and speak of the partnership relation and of the agency, liabilities, claims and duties which it involves—which give effect to it as a relation of good faith—not of a contract of *societas*. We think of the claims and duties involved in a fiduciary relation and of the legal incidents that give effect to trusteeship or executorship as a relation of good faith, not of the implications of the declaration of will involved in accepting or declaring a trust or qualifying as executor. We do not ask what are the logical deductions from the will of the parties involved in a sale of land. We ask what incidents attach in equity when the vendor-purchaser relation arises. We do not think of giving effect to the will of the parties to a contract of hypothecation. We consider what incidents

---

[1] See Adams, *The Origin of the English Constitution*, chap. 5 (1912).

are involved in the relation of mortgagor and mortgagee and the reciprocal claims and duties that give effect thereto.

We must remember that the analogy which was ever before the lawyers and judges of the formative period of our law, the typical social and legal institution of the time, was the relation of lord and man, still represented in our law by the relation of landlord and tenant. Continual resort to this analogy, consciously or subconsciously, has made the idea of relation the central idea in our traditional mode of juristic thought. In public law the seventeenth and eighteenth centuries sought to substitute the Romanist idea of contract borrowed from Continental publicists[1]. In private law the eighteenth century, with its contempt for the Middle Ages, and the nineteenth century, with its desire to see all things in terms of the maximum of individual self-assertion, sought continually to restate the theory of our institutions and doctrines in terms of contract or of will. Thus, for a time we tried vainly to state the law of public service or of public utilities in terms of a contract of transportation, so that a generation ago some American courts were calling a telephone company a common carrier of messages and an electric-light and power company a common carrier of electric current and were thinking of the conduct of their enterprizes by these companies and of the giving of free passes by railroad corporations in terms of Mr Barkis giving a free ride to a small boy or of the contracts which he might make with his patrons[2]. The signal failure of the contract theory of this subject and the development of a law of public utilities on a relational theory are significant proofs of the vitality of the common law.

No relational analogy was at hand in the formative period of Roman law. The Roman household was organized on the basis of authority, not on the basis of a relation involving reciprocal rights and duties. When the foundations of the modern

[1] Blackstone, *Commentaries*, 1, 234–236. In American legal literature this goes back to Locke, *Two Treatises of Civil Government*, Bk 11, ch. 7 (1690), which proceeds on ideas of natural law derived from Roman jurists through sixteenth-century discussions that go back to medieval controversies between emperor or king and church. In American juristic thought this current joins in the eighteenth century with Continental natural-law political philosophy.

[2] See Wyman, "Business Policies Inconsistent with Public Employment," 20 *Harvard Law Rev.* 511 (1907).

Roman law were laid jurists believed that they could do no more than interpret and apply the authoritative Roman texts. Hence the analogies used were Roman analogies drawn from the *Corpus Juris*. Accordingly while common-law ways of thinking were determined by the analogies of the medieval, feudal, relationally organized society in which they arose, the ways of thinking in the modern Roman law were determined by the analogies of the city-state political society of heads of households in the stage of the strict law. These ways of thinking were liberalized and idealized in the classical period of Roman law—from the first to the third century—and again during the reign of the law-of-nature school in the seventeenth and eighteenth centuries. But the claims and duties of free men, Roman citizens and heads of households, owning adjoining homesteads, encountering each other in the streets and entering into undertakings toward each other in the various activities of life, shaped Roman juristic thought and led Roman jurists and hence the Romanists of today to think and speak of letting and sale and mandate and contract of partnership as naturally as the reciprocal rights and duties of men in relations, claiming this or that against each other as an incident of the relation, shaped English legal thought and led the common-law jurist to think and speak of landlord and tenant, vendor and purchaser, principal and agent and the partnership relation. It is noteworthy that in our law of sales of chattels, shaped by the law merchant and along the lines of the Continental Romanized commercial law through the influence of nineteenth-century text-writers[1], we speak of the contract of sale and of what it implies. In the law of sales of land, governed by the common law and developed by equity on common-law lines, we think and speak of the relation of vendor and purchaser. The will theory of legal transaction as an idea of contract, upon which the political interpretation builds, is not a universal idea of all law. It is relative to Roman law. It is a generalization from doctrines expressing the problem which chiefly concerned Roman lawyers

[1] The text-book of widest influence was Benjamin on Sales. Benjamin was by original training a civilian and spent the formative portion of his legal life in the practice of law in Louisiana at a time when the law of that state was essentially French.

in the beginnings of Roman juristic activity—the problem of
adjusting the conflicting claims of heads of households exercising
authority within their households and jealous of authority
without—interpreted in terms of the juristic problem of the
nineteenth century.

Moreover the generalization of progress from status to contract, understood as a progress from limitations of freedom or
liabilities existing or imposed independently of will toward a
complete freedom of contract and liability only for willed undertakings or culpable conduct, is refuted by the whole course of
development of the law, whether by legislation or by judicial
decision, in the last generation, unless indeed we have been
progressing backward. We must not omit to notice that Maine
was more cautious than his followers. He was willing to limit
status to its Roman sense of personal condition and to exclude
relations resulting from legal transactions. Also he qualified
his formula by saying that the movement of progressive societies
had been "hitherto" a movement from status to contract. Yet
he considered this observed orbit of progress as indicating
sufficiently a general law of legal development[1], and his followers
conceiving that history, or as it came to be called, evolution,
was progress and was subject to discoverable laws, eliminated
the qualification. Likewise, carrying the second half of his
formula to its logical conclusion, they eliminated the qualification which he attached to the term status. In America, at least,
it was taken for gospel that law was moving and must move in
the direction of abstract individual self-determination by free
contract and liability only for undertakings and for fault. One
may speak with less assurance as to British thought on this
subject since the courts had no occasion to apply the generaliza-

---

[1] "The word status may be usefully employed to construct a formula
expressing the law of progress thus indicated which, whatever its value,
seems to me to be sufficiently indicated. All the forms of status taken notice
of in the law of persons were derived from, and to some extent are still
coloured by, the powers and privileges anciently residing in the family. If,
then, we employ status, agreeably with the usage of the best writers, to
signify these personal conditions only, and avoid applying the term to such
conditions as are the immediate or remote result of agreement, we may say
that the movement of the progressive societies has hitherto been a movement
from status to contract." *Ancient Law*, last paragraph of chap. 5.

tion in interpreting a bill of rights and applying it to social legislation. But Miller's denunciation of the Irish land legislation of the eighties as reversing "the natural order of growth" and his prophecy that its repeal was inevitable are at least suggestive[1]. British legislation since 1865 and American legislation since 1890 give Diogenes' answer to such propositions. When we reflect, however, that this interpretation of Maine's formula was the accepted legal science of the last generation, we may understand why American state courts from 1890 to 1910 were so confidently dogmatic in holding modern social legislation to be unconstitutional.

Since Maine's generalization was formulated and was interpreted by his followers, limitation of free contract and imposition of duties and liabilities as incidents of relations instead of exclusively as the consequences of manifested will, have gone forward steadily both in judicial decision and in legislation. If we compare the English decisions as to covenants not to compete or not to enter the service of a competitor rendered between 1870 and 1890 with those rendered since 1910 the change in the direction of restriction of the power to bind oneself by such a covenant is striking. The whole doctrine as to contracts not to exercise the calling for which one has trained himself has taken a new turn within a decade[2]. Sir George Jessel's proposition, that public policy demands more than anything else that men be allowed to contract freely and that the contracts which they make freely be enforced[3], is no longer an expression of the judicial attitude toward such covenants. Again the growth of a law of public utilities in which doctrines flow not from the undertakings or professings of the entity engaging in public service but from the requirements of the service, which are taken to fix the incidental duties attaching to the calling, tells the same story[4]. In America, also, the

[1] *Lectures on the Philosophy of Law*, 71–73 (1884).
[2] *Attwood v. Lamont*, [1920] 3 K.B. 571, 593.
[3] *Printing and Numerical Registering Co. v. Sampson*, 19 Eq. 462, 465 (1875). Compare *Bauer v. O'Donnell*, 229 *United States Reports*, 1 (1912).
[4] In England this has been the work of legislation. In the United States there has been a judicial development. In each case the development has been upon common-law lines. See Wyman, *The Special Law Governing Public Service Corporations*, 1, §§ 1–14, 20, 27, 32–42 (1911).

decisions as to warranties in policies of insurance, restricting
freedom of contract in the relation of insurer and insured either
avowedly or ׀·y strained interpretation, and the decisions treating
insurance as a public calling have gone along with legislative
regulation of the contracts which insurers may make and point
in a direction quite opposite to what had been regarded as the
course of legal development[1].

Social legislation has gone even further. Statutes restricting
the power of a husband to mortgage household goods or assign
wages without the consent of his wife have tied down the *ius
disponendi*[2]. Workmen's compensation legislation has imposed
liability without regard to fault. Truck acts have forbidden
payment of employees by orders on company stores and have
required payment of wages in cash. It is true that a workmen's
compensation act was held unconstitutional by the New York
Court of Appeals in 1911[3] and that a minority of the Supreme
Court of the United States considered such legislation unconstitutional in 1920[4]. It is true also that the truck acts were
held unreasonable and unconstitutional by a line of state
decisions between 1886 and 1910[5]. But the opposition of the
courts to such legislation grew out of their acceptance of the
doctrine that the evolution of law was a progress from status to
contract and it broke down in the second decade of the present
century. This opposition was not due to class bias or economic
associations or social relations of the judges nor to sinister

[1] See my paper, "The End of Law as Developed in Legal Rules and
Doctrines," 27 *Harvard Law Rev.* 195, 225; *New York Life Ins. Co.* v.
Hardison, 199 *Massachusetts Reports*, 190 (1908); *Fidelity Mutual Ins. Co.*
v. *Miazza*, 93 *Mississippi Reports*, 18 (1908); *Attorney General* v. *Fireman's
Ins. Co.*, 74 *New Jersey Equity Reports*, 372 (1909); *Boston Ice Co.* v. *Boston
and M. R. Co.*, 77 *New Hampshire Reports*, 6 (1914); *John Hancock Mutual
Life Ins. Co.* v. *Warren*, 181 *United States Reports*, 73 (1901); *Orient Ins. Co.*
v. *Daggs*, 172 *United States Reports*, 557 (1899); *Port Blakely M. Co.* v.
Springfield Ins. Co., 59 *Washington Reports*, 501 (1910). In the case last cited
a dissenting judge observed that the decision, under the guise of "interpretation," wipes out the law of warranty as it formerly existed in connection
with insurance.

[2] *Illinois, Rev. Stat.* 1909, chap. 95, § 24; *Massachusetts, Acts of* 1908,
chap. 605. Compare New Zealand Family Protection Act, 1908.

[3] *Ives* v. *South Buffalo R. Co.*, 201 *New York Reports*, 271 (1911).

[4] *Arizona Copper Co.* v. *Hammer*, 250 *United States Reports*, 400, 433,
440 (1920).

[5] See my paper, "Liberty of Contract," 18 *Yale Law Journ.* 454.

influences brought to bear upon them, as was assumed so freely in the American presidential campaign of 1912, when such decisions were in issue. The judges were imbued with a genuine faith in the tenets of the historical school, especially the political interpretation and the doctrine of progress from status to contract. Hence it seemed to them that the constitutional requirement of due process of law was violated by legislative attempts to restore status and restrict the contractual powers of free men by enacting that men of full age and sound mind in particular callings should not be able to make agreements which other men might make freely. The federal census of 1920 shows that the United States has passed definitely from a preponderantly rural and agricultural to a preponderantly urban and industrial civilization. The social wants of twentieth-century America have driven the courts in one way or another to uphold such legislation and have convinced us reluctantly that the law may grow and for a time must grow in a different direction from what we had considered its fixed and inevitable orbit[1].

Indeed the political interpretation was put to a thorough test by the conscientious logical application of it as an interpretation of due process of law made by American state courts in three decades of struggle with state legislatures. For this application brought out an inconsistency between the doctrine of progress from status to contract, as the last generation understood it, and the principles of equity which had developed in our law, especially in the seventeenth and eighteenth centuries. The state courts held for two decades that legislative imposition of contractual incapacities in the relation of employer and employee was arbitrary and hence unconstitutional. But there were existing incapacities with which they did not think of interfering. The surviving common-law incapacities could be idealized as "natural incapacities." Usury laws were not so easy to explain. But courts said that there had been such laws from the beginnings of American legislation, and some, ignorant of

[1] See *Noble State Bank* v. *Haskell*, 219 *United States Reports*, 104 (1911); *Chicago R. Co.* v. *McGuire*, 219 *United States Reports*, 549, 566–575 (1911).

English law-making, that they were immemorial and universal[1]. In other words, they were familiar historically and hence reasonable. There remained equitable restrictions on free contract, the doctrine as to penalties, the refusal to allow the holder of a penal bond to recover more than the actual damages, the doctrine of redemption of mortgaged property after the condition had become absolute, the rule against clogging the equity of redemption, the rules as to sailors' contracts and sales by reversioners. An eighteenth-century chancellor had explained these by saying that necessitous persons were not free. But the courts shrank from so recognizing the facts of industrial employment in the face of the abstract freedom which they had set up as an ideal. The best they could say was that the equitable incapacities also were historical[2]. This amounted to holding that the legislature was unable to create new contractual incapacities; that the lines had been drawn forever in the seventeenth and eighteenth centuries and that no new type of disability could be recognized. Nor did it matter that the underlying principle of these new statutory disabilities was the same as that underlying the disabilities imposed by equity. Anything that savoured of a status of labourer was contrary to the right line of legal progress and was unreasonable. The most the legislature could do was to abolish such things as for example in Married Women's Acts. The fallacy of the courts in these cases will not have escaped you. A statute forbidding contracts to accept wages in the form of orders on a company store did not classify the labourer with the infant, the lunatic and the felon[3]. It defined an incident of a relation freely entered into and so came within Maine's qualification. But in the political interpretation freedom meant an abstract freedom—the abstract idea of insuring a maximum of individual self assertion as the

---

[1] "The right to regulate the rate of interest existed at the time the constitution was adopted, and cannot therefore be considered as either an abridgment or restraint upon the rights of the citizen guaranteed by the constitution. The power to pass usury laws exists by immemorial usage; but such is not the case with such laws as we are now considering." *State* v. *Goodwill*, 33 *West Virginia Reports*, 179 (1889).

[2] See *State* v. *Loomis*, 115 *Missouri Reports*, 307 (1890).

[3] The court made this statement in *State* v. *Haun*, 61 *Kansas Reports*, 146, 161 (1900).

ideal by which all things legal were to be judged. Accordingly the courts saw rightly enough that if the doctrine was to be a guide, they must carry it out to its conclusion. By doing so rigorously they disproved the political interpretation as an interpretation of Anglo-American legal history.

Looking back at the reign of the political interpretation, we may perceive two respects in which it failed to satisfy at the end of the last and at the beginning of the present century, after general acceptance for a generation. In the first place it was a negative juristic theory, carrying to the limit the idea of the historical school that nothing was to be created—that legislation was futile. In the hands of common-law lawyers this became a conviction that an idealized form of the common law was the legal order of nature and led to an excessive development of the doctrine of strictly construing statutes in derogation of the common law and to strained interpretations in the direction of holding new legislation to be merely declaratory of traditional rules. Thus American state courts laid down dogmatically that general principles of constitutional law forbade legislative adoption of the theory of the *forum laesae civitatis* as the basis of jurisdiction over crimes[1]. They kept back the full legal emancipation of married women for fifty years by holding the statutes rigidly to the precisely detailed changes which they made in express terms rigidly construed[2]. They kept American legal procedure in a backward state for half a century by reading into codes of procedure an idealized system of actions on a historico-analytical basis[3]. They even began to undo the work of the uniform commercial laws by treating them in each state as declaratory of the local course of judicial decision prior to the statutes and so as perpetuating the condition which they were meant to relieve[4]. Secondly it rejected all

---

[1] *State* v. *Carter*, 41 *New Jersey Law Reports*, 499, 501–503 (1859).
[2] I have discussed this phenomenon in "Common Law and Legislation," 21 *Harvard Law Rev.* 383. See Carter, *Law; Its Origin, Growth and Function*, 308–309.
[3] A leading case was *Supervisors* v. *Decker*, 30 *Wisconsin Reports*, 624, 626–627, 629–630 (1872), now happily overruled by *Bruheim* v. *Stratton*, 145 *Wisconsin Reports*, 271 (1911).
[4] For recent examples, see Chafee, "Progress of the Law: Bills and Notes," 33 *Harvard Law Rev.* 225, *passim* (1919).

criticism of legal institutions and rules and doctrines other than a historico-analytical criticism of the law in terms of itself. This attitude has its counterpart in history-writing at large during the same period. "To conceive of history as evolution and progress," says Croce, "implies accepting it as necessary in all its parts and therefore denying validity to judgments upon it[1]." The rational is real and the real is rational. Hence it is futile to criticize legal institutions or to attempt to improve them by legislation[2]. The progressive unfolding of the idea must be our reliance. Juristic or legislative attempts to hasten or to direct the process were vain. Historical fatalism became juristic pessimism. Those who sought to improve the law were branded as harmless Utopians or as belated representatives of the eighteenth century.

What this meant in action is well illustrated in the attitude of the last century toward the doctrine of consideration. Lord Mansfield came very near ridding us of it and establishing that a promise made as a business transaction in the course of business was legally enforceable as such without more[3]. But before his liberal conception of contract could become fixed in the law the reaction from constructive reshaping of legal materials had set in. When the nineteenth-century legal historians studied the subject it was not in the spirit of showing that the needs or wants that gave rise to the doctrine had been satisfied long ago, and that it no longer served a useful purpose, but in order to find an idea of consideration by which the whole future development of the law of contracts must be governed. They did not criticize it. They fortified it and enabled it to survive so that, although slowly crumbling and loaded with exceptions and analytical anomalies, it remains a serious barrier in the way of security of transactions. It is disquieting to think that when letters of credit became an important instrument in export and in manufacturing during the late war this doctrine imposed serious difficulties in the way of legal recognition of the general course of practice of the business world[4] and that

---

[1] *Storia della storiografia Italiana nel secolo decimonono*, I, 26.
[2] Burdick, "A Revival of Benthamite Codification," 10 *Columbia Law Rev.* 118, 123, 125–126 (1910).
[3] *Pillans* v. *Van Mierop*, 3 Burr. 1663 (1765).
[4] Hershey, "Letters of Credit," 32 *Harvard Law Rev.* 1 (1918).

the theory by which American courts have sought to get around some of these difficulties is not available in England, as authoritatively determined by the House of Lords[1]. Such indifference to the practical functioning of the legal system cannot endure. More than anything else the abandonment of the jurist's function, the juristic pessimism, involved in the idea of the futility of legislation and the futility of criticism, brought about the general revolt from the historical school at the end of the last century and the beginning of the present century. "In its application to the social sciences," said Saleilles in 1902, "history ought to become a creative force. The historical school stopped half way[2]." In that it showed itself impotent to furnish a creative method, he added, it ceased to be a school of jurists. Likewise it was an attempt to interpret Australian social legislation that led Jethro Brown in 1912 to turn from the orthodox English historical-analytical jurisprudence toward a revival of philosophical jurisprudence[3].

No doubt eighteenth-century jurists had gone too far in assuming that legal systems which were the result of a long historical development or a long process of working with or upon old materials might be wholly reconstructed at pleasure in accord with abstract principles of right. But what may be done by an enlightened judicial policy of shaping the law to an ideal which corresponds to social demands is shown by the absorptions of equity into the law under Lord Mansfield, the development of the common counts on the principle of preventing unjust enrichment of one at the expense of another, the taking over of the law merchant, the judicial development of mercantile institutions and usages, and the making over of seventeenth-century English law into a common law of America by means of the doctrine that the common law of England was in force only so far as it was applicable to American conditions and American institutions. Also there are examples of successful taking over of a whole body of law at one stroke, especially where the common interests of a people with diverse and inadequate local laws have come to call for legal unity. The

---

[1] *Dunlop Pneumatic Tyre Co.* v. *Selfridge*, [1915] A.C. 847.
[2] "L'École historique et droit naturel," *Revue trimestrielle de droit civil*, I, 90, 94 (1902).
[3] *Underlying Principles of Modern Legislation*, 64–67 (1912).

reception of Roman law in Western Europe, the reception of nineteenth-century Continental law in Japan, the Anglo-Indian codes, and the almost verbatim reception of the French civil code in many different lands show that there is more to be said for the faith of the law-of-nature school than we have been wont to perceive. In the reaction from the law-of-nature theory the historical school went too far in the other direction and sought to exclude development and improvement of the law from the field of conscious human effort.

On the other hand we must put many important achievements to the credit of the second phase of the historical school. It laid the foundations of a sound comparative legal history in place of the brilliant superficiality of the eighteenth-century universal legal history in terms of rational conjecture. It gave us a sounder and more critical history of Roman law, of Germanic law and of English law. For the philological and legal archaeological study of these bodies of law, with no ethical idea to prejudice it and conducted with a high feeling for the intrinsic value of the original sources and a conviction that whatever was discovered historically must be right because it represented the unfolding of the idea, so that we did not need to trouble ourselves about what was found but only to find what was there to be found—this attitude led to the rejection of much legal pseudo-history which had come down from the eighteenth century. In its unification of jurisprudence and politics, if it was not the actual forerunner of the unification of the social sciences which is going on today, at least it kept alive one connection of jurisprudence when nearly all had been dissolved. Finally through its attempt to generalize the phenomena of primitive law and of developed systems by a theory of custom it led to the idea of the legal order as part of a wider social control from which it cannot be dissociated. For the historical school thought of the legal order not as the whole nor as a wholly self-sufficient part of social control but as one phase of it, merging back into an undifferentiated religion, morals and law. This way of thinking did much to help break down the conception of law as something existing of itself and for itself and to be measured by itself; it prepared the way for the functional attitude of the legal science of today.

IV

ETHNOLOGICAL AND BIOLOGICAL
INTERPRETATIONS

A CONDITION of philosophical stagnation marks the second half of the nineteenth century. The sharp contrasts of ideals that went along with and immediately followed the French Revolution challenged philosophers and impelled them to seek to reconcile radicalism and tradition, rationalism and faith, intelligence and will or to organize the phenomena of society and of history in terms of one or the other. When these contrasts ceased for the time being to challenge attention because of the general setting up of a regime of constitutional political equilibrium and economic stability, interest shifted on the one hand to the physical and biological sciences, which were related directly to industry and economic prosperity, and on the other hand to an empirical political and social science. For fifty years philosophy as such was under a cloud. Such movements always affect jurisprudence somewhat later than related social sciences because lawyers respond cautiously to new tendencies through solicitude for the social interest in the general security and fear of impairing the stability of the legal order. But in the last third of the nineteenth century the abandonment of philosophy had gone so far that the philosophical jurists either had been swallowed up in the dominant historical school or had disappeared. Outside of Italy the nineteenth-century philosophical school substantially came to an end. The last noteworthy book from this standpoint appeared in 1882[1]. In the same year the successor of Ahrens at Brussels did homage to historical jurisprudence for his fief of natural law[2]. In 1887, 1888 and 1889, when three French jurists successively ventured modest philosophical introductions to law they felt bound to write apologetic

---

[1] Lasson, *Lehrbuch der Rechtsphilosophie*; Boistel, *Cours de philosophie du droit* (1899) is a new edition of a work written in 1870.
[2] Prins, *La philosophie du droit et l'école historique*.

prefaces[1]. In 1898 a pupil and successor of Lorimer began to teach analytical jurisprudence at Edinburgh[2]. Patronizing disparagement of philosophy became the rule. As Kohler puts it, "to speak of the philosophy of law passed for obsolete and old-fashioned[3]." The writing of legal history began more and more to be a mere collection of facts, all equally significant and equally insignificant. In jurisprudence and in politics a descriptive analytical method prevailed. The details of legal and political institutions were described in accordance with an analysis drawn from the institutions themselves, and they were described so faithfully as they stood in detail on a given day that they had ceased so to stand before the book was off the press. The abdication of the jurist's function by the historical school and the doctrine of the futility of criticism had borne fruit. To quote Kohler once more: "The exposition of a passage in the praetor's edict was held more important than investigation of the laws of legal development....The rule of law became an implacable tyrant. The philosophical jurist was gagged[4]."

Yet jurists did not wholly give over philosophical activity. The need of reconciling stability and change was always with them, even when the exclusive cult of stability was at its height. Moreover toward the end of the century dissatisfaction with the dominant historical school was constantly increasing and the pressure of new interests was continually more manifest both in judicial decision and in social legislation. Thus the transition from the metaphysical jurisprudence of the nineteenth century to the social philosophical jurisprudence of today required some sort of philosophical bridge. The first attempts at such a bridge were made by means of ethnology and biology.

Three circumstances contributed successively to turn juristic thinking to race as a factor in legal development and to suggest

---

[1] "The study of these principles, in which France was deeply interested a hundred years ago, seems abandoned or at least much neglected today. But it is worthy of attention from several points of view." Courcelles-Seneuil, *Préparation à l'étude du droit*, preface (1887). Compare Beaussire, *Les principes du droit*, preface (1888); Vareilles-Sommières, *Les principes fondamentaux du droit*, preface (1889).

[2] Miller, *Jurisprudence, Its Place in the New Curriculum*, 10 (1898).

[3] *Lehrbuch der Rechtsphilosophie*, 6 (1909).

[4] *Ibid.*

the organic analogy: the rise of positivism and consequent development of a science of society, the rise of biological science and consequent influence of biology upon all contemporary thinking, and the rise of modern psychology and consequent study of group and of race psychology. The founder of positivism was also the founder of a science treating of social phenomena to which unhappily he gave the barbarous name of sociology. The name has affected many so unfavourably that they have not been inclined to give consideration to the thing named. Likewise the subject matter had been pre-empted in part in small parcels by a group of special independent social sciences, after the manner of the nineteenth century which, also after the manner of that century, refused to think of themselves as social and affected to proceed on a metaphysical foundation of abstract individual freedom. Likewise the words "sociology" and "social" troubled many because they suggested "socialism," a much-embracing word of sinister connotations then as now, although the chief English exponent of sociology in the last century was an orthodox individualist of an extreme type. Partly for these reasons the science of society made no great progress for some time. But what held it back chiefly was the turn given it at first by the mental bent of its founder.

Comte was a mathematician and drew his analogies largely from mathematical physics and from astronomy. Indeed, as has been pointed out more than once, the book that governed men's imaginations when his ideas were formative was the *Mécanique céleste* of Laplace[1]. Thus the first sociology was a mechanical social science; an attempt to find by observation and to verify mechanical laws, analogous to those governing the movements of heavenly bodies, by which social phenomena were no less inexorably governed. Such a mode of thought accorded well with the juristic ideas of the historical school, especially in its second phase, so that when the metaphysical ideas of that school became out of fashion, some of its adherents, who perceived that a philosophical foundation was needed for their historico-analytical ideas, turned eagerly to positivism. They were much at home therein, for, as many critics have

[1] See Small, *The Meaning of Social Science*, 74.

observed, there was a persistent Hegelian element in the positivism
of the last quarter of the nineteenth century[1]. Thus for a
season we got attempts at positivist or sociological legal history
and mechanical sociological jurisprudence of what is at bottom
a Hegelian type. For not only was the mechanical sociology
as fatalist as the metaphysical history but the positivist jurists
were either pupils of or got their legal materials from the
historical jurists and so took them as seen through Hegelian
spectacles.

Mechanical sociology achieved nothing in jurisprudence
beyond serving as a forerunner[2]. Hence it has been easy for the
undiscriminating to criticize all the phases of sociological jurisprudence which have followed, assuming that they are or that
they must be identical therewith[3]. One will fail to understand
much in the legal science of today if he makes such an assumption.
But it is enough for our present purpose that a party of jurists
had been set to thinking about something else than reconciling
of conflicting individual wills and to talking of some other idea
than abstract individual freedom. This, at any rate, was a
distinct gain.

A second generation of sociologists was influenced by the rise
of biological science and in particular by Darwin. It is not too
much to say that Darwin furnished the phrases and provided
the analogies and suggested the lines of thought for that generation as decisively as Laplace had done for its predecessors. In
Spencer, who began to write on social science before Darwin,
we may trace the change as one of terminology, in a replacing
of mechanical by biological analogies. But Spencer's sociology
remained mechanical in all but terminology to the end. Moreover the idea of evolution made real headway slowly in biology
itself as against a tendency to force the phenomena of life into
scholastic or metaphysically-organized classifications and to
formulate laws of development on the basis of meagre data and

[1] E.g. Croce, *Storia della storiografia Italiana*, ii, 172–173.
[2] See Berolzheimer, *System der Rechts- und Wirthschaftsphilosophie*,
ii, 384 (1905).
[3] See Charmont, *La renaissance du droit naturel*, chap. 5 (1910); Kor-
kunov, *General Theory of Law*, transl. by Hastings, 265–266 (written in 1887);
Berolzheimer, *System der Rechts- und Wirthschaftsphilosophie*, ii, § 44 (1905).

in closed philosophical systems. The analogy of physical laws and of the movements of the planets gave way to an analogy of less known biological laws. Organic evolution, the analogy of the organic and the "super-organic," and applications of the struggle for existence and the survival of the fittest to social phenomena are the *differentiae* of the biological sociology and of sociological jurisprudence in its biological stage. In its net results the biological sociology did no more than carry forward the work of preparation begun by the mechanical sociology. Hence the one is open to the stock criticisms directed against the other and criticism of either or of both may serve easily for criticism of the sociological jurisprudence of today, if we assume that the same name must always cover the same content, that all phases of sociological jurisprudence are convertible and that it is impossible for a science to develop to the extent of radical improvement in its methods within a generation[1].

Later the rise of psychology exerted a profound influence upon sociology and upon sociological jurisprudence, which is still at work. Gierke turned the attention of jurists toward groups as something more than aggregates of individuals and on their legal side, when recognized legally, something more than legal fictions[2]. Thus jurisprudence and politics were brought into relation with group psychology and folk psychology. Tarde discovered a factor of the first moment in the shaping of legal materials and in the eking out of a body of legal rules and doctrines by materials drawn from without, and formulated the laws of imitation upon a philosophical as well as a psychological foundation[3]. Ward preached the efficacy of effort and urged

[1] See Tanon, *L'Évolution de droit et la conscience sociale*, 3rd ed. 180–189 (1911); Tourtoulon, *Principes philosophiques de l'histoire du droit*, 80–173 (1908); Berolzheimer, *System der Rechts- und Wirthschaftsphilosophie*, II, §§ 47, 51 (1905).

[2] "What man is he owes to the union of man with man. The possibility of creating associations, which not only enhance the power of those who live contemporaneously but, above all, through their permanence, surviving the personality of the individual, bind the past of the race to those to come, gives us the possibility of the development of history." Gierke, *Deutsche Genossenschaftsrecht*, I, I (1868). See also *Das Wesen der menschlichen Verbände*, 33–34.

[3] Tarde, *Laws of Imitation*, transl. by Parsons, 2–3, 11–13, 14–15, 310–320 (written 1890); Tarde, *Les transformations du droit* (1894, 6th ed. 1909).

the decisive rôle of the psychic factors of civilization[1]. Thus a wide breach was made in the juristic dogma of the historical school. In the meantime a revival of philosophy of law began, resulting in the social-philosophical jurisprudence of today. With the beginning of the present century came unification of the methods of sociology[2], unification of the social sciences[3], the functional attitude—consideration of the workings of law more than of its abstract content—the attitude of looking on law as a social institution which may be improved by intelligent human effort, and belief that it is the duty of jurists to discover the most effective means of directing and furthering such effort. These things have come to be the accepted creed of sociological jurists and in increasing measure are becoming the creed of all jurists. What we shall be looking at is a stage in this development. Experiments in psychological forms of ethnological interpretation are a link between the nineteenth-century search for a single all-explaining formula of legal development and the recognition of a plurality of factors which marks the juristic thought of today.

It is convenient to distinguish two main types of these transitional interpretations—the ethnological and the biological. The former interprets law and legal history in terms of race spirit or race psychology or race institutions, which in the systems of positivists are regarded usually as resulting from physical environment. The latter interprets them in terms of the Darwinian natural selection—in terms of struggle for existence and survival of the fittest. The ethnological type came first and served as a connecting link between Hegel and the positivists, between the nineteenth-century philosophical or metaphysical jurists and sociological jurisprudence. Accordingly it takes three forms. In the first form it is idealistic. A race idea is unfolding in the development of the legal institutions of this or that people or, more generally, the idea is looked at

---

[1] *Dynamic Sociology*, I, 468–472 (1883); *The Psychic Factors of Civilization*, 120 (1901); *Applied Sociology*, 13 (1906).
[2] Ward, *Contemporary Sociology*, reprint of papers in 7 *American Journal of Sociology*, 475, 629, 749; Ward, *Pure Sociology*, 14 (1903).
[3] Ward, *Pure Sociology*, 12–14 (1903); Small, *General Sociology*, 91 (1905); Small, *The Meaning of Social Science*, 87 (1910).

from a special point of view as that of the race in whose spirit it is unfolding. In a second form it is psychological. Law is taken to be an expression of the character, mentality or temperament of the race in whose social institutions it has developed. In a third form it is positivist. Law is ultimately a product of the external physical causes which have determined the character, mentality and temperament of the races in which legal systems have developed. It is immediately a product of race character and temperament arising from conflict of instincts and the need of harmonizing them in action if the race is to endure.

We may trace the first form back to Hegel. In his philosophy of right and law (1820) he suggested an interpretation of legal history by conceiving the idea in terms of particular races or nations[1]. History was the march of the spirit in the world and so legal history the march of freedom in civil relations. If we looked simply at legal or political history, it moved now through this institution and now through that. But looking at all history in a very wide survey, we might say that it moved now through this race and now through that. Babylon, Egypt, Persia, Greece, Rome, the Germanic peoples of Western Europe were successively the vehicles through which the idea realized itself. Nothing else had power against this march of the idea in the world[2]. This conception of Hegel's, taken over by jurists, gave us an idealistic ethnological interpretation.

One of the first attempts at applying this interpretation, at doing more than sketching the broad lines of a universal legal history from this standpoint, was made by Jhering in connection with the beginnings of Roman law[3]. It is familiar to English and American students through Muirhead's adoption of it in

[1] "§ 346....A single principle, involved in its geographical and anthropological existence is to be attributed to each people. § 347. The accomplishing of a stage of development, through the process characteristic of the self-developing self-consciousness of the world spirit, belongs to the people whose natural principle is one of these stages of development. This people is dominant for a given epoch in the history of the world...." *Grundlinien der Philosophie des Rechts*, §§ 346-347.

[2] "In contrast with the absolute power of this people to be the bearer of the current phase in the development of the world spirit, the spirits of other peoples are void of power." *Id.* § 347.

[3] *Geist des römischen Rechts*, I, § 19 (1852), 4th ed. I, 310.

his almost classical exposition[1]. Jhering pointed out a dualism in the old Roman law in that two systems, a religious system and a profane system, existed side by side. On the one hand there was the religious system of *fas*, with fire and water for its symbol, with Numa for its representative, with a religious marriage by *confarreatio*, with religious legal transactions of *sacramentum, sponsio, foedus*, with a religious legal procedure in the *legis actio sacramento* and a religious idea of punishment as expiation or purification in *sacratio* and sacrificial execution. On the other hand there was the profane system of *ius*, with the spear and the strong hand for its symbols, with Romulus for its representative, with acquisition by purchase as its marriage, with publicly witnessed legal transactions of *mancipium* and *nexum*, with a legal procedure founded on self-help and a system of penalties by way of composition. In other words, one relied on religious sanctions, had a religious symbol, was represented by a religious king, purported to rest on a divine basis; the other relied on force, had military symbols, was represented by a military king, and purported to rest on the political authority of the Roman people. The suggestion was that the one was Sabine, the other Roman. But this dualism is by no means peculiar to the beginnings of Roman legal institutions. It may be found, for that matter, in the Anglo-Saxon laws. With respect to them one might easily work out an ingenious parallel of a Christian system side by side with a profane system; of a reliance on exhortations addressed by the king to his subjects as pious Christians[2] and a reliance on threats of employing armed force[3]; of a crude division of jurisdiction between church and state, and a series of religious institutions on the one hand and parallel lay legal institutions on the other hand. Religion and law are co-ordinate agencies of social control in a certain stage of social development. One is the agency

---

[1] *Historical Introduction to the Private Law of Rome*, § 1 (1886).

[2] Also one might refer to the prefixing of the Ten Commandments, extracts from Exodus and extracts from the New Testament by way of introduction to Alfred's Laws. Liebermann, *Gesetze der Angelsachsen*, I, 26–46. Also the prologue to Ine's Laws, *id*. 89.

[3] E.g. *Judicia Civitatis Lundoniae*, VIII, 2; Liebermann, *Gesetze der Angelsachsen*, I, 178.

of social control in a kin-organized society, the other in a politically organized society. In a stage of transition they are more or less co-ordinate. With the break-down of kin-organization because of the rise of a non-gentile population, the law takes over and absorbs the chief religious institutions of social control. Thus we get a dualism in the beginnings of the legal order which gradually disappears. There is no need to invoke ethnical dualism in the old city of Rome to explain a phenomenon so evidently due to general causes which produced like results in like stages of legal development among other peoples where no hypothesis of two-fold racial composition will serve us. This particular ethnological interpretation was soon abandoned.

Dahn in 1878 gave a new direction to the idealistic ethnological interpretation. He noted the tendency of philosophers of law who were not lawyers to put specious reasons behind legal institutions and legal doctrines as they were rather than to criticize them on a philosophical basis, and the tendency of other philosophers of law to leave the actual law wholly out of account. These two tendencies had much to do with bringing philosophical jurisprudence into disrepute in the latter part of the nineteenth century. Seeing that the metaphysical method had ceased to be of value, he proposed a new and broader basis for legal philosophy. "A philosophy of law," he said, "which shall be more than a collection of phrases must begin with speculative valuation of the results of the historical school and with the setting up of a legal philosophical edifice on the basis of comparative legal history, folk psychology and ethnology[1]." We have here on the one hand an attempt to bring the historical and the philosophical methods together on a better basis than the conventional reconciliation that history verifies the metaphysical deduction or metaphysics demonstrates what history discovers. We have also, on the other hand, a movement in the sociological direction, involving a comparative legal history with a social-psychological and anthropological background—a legal history that is not to be merely doctrinal or politico-institutional, comparing abstract legal propositions or abstract politico-legal

[1] *Rechtsphilosophische Studien*, 288.

institutions, but is to rest on generalizations from the observed phenomena of folk psychology and of the character, civilization and environment of peoples. Each of these suggestions found followers. The idealistic ethnological interpretation took a psychological turn. The positivist ethnological interpretation, which already had been foreshadowed by Post in 1876[1], was given a comparative basis.

In its psychological form the ethnological interpretation postulates a certain legal genius or type of mind for each people and seeks to explain legal history and the phenomena of legal systems accordingly. In the hands of philosophers it has been idealistic: the legal genius or the spirit of each people has mani-fested itself in the unfolding of some idea by which the legal history of that people and its legal institutions may be explained. Carle made a notable attempt to sketch the law of the modern world in terms of English and French and German and Italian legal ideas, expressing the psychology of these several peoples, and running back to likeness or difference of race or to race fusions[2]. Fouillée explained the law of modern Europe in terms of the spirit of the different peoples of today, urging an inter-pretation of French law and of the influence of the French civil code in terms of the spirit of the French[3]. Recently this inter-pretation has been urged once more, this time on a social-psychological basis, by McDougall[4]. Divested of its meta-physical aspects in its latest form, it sees a special character or temperament or predisposition in each race which manifests itself, among other things, in the social and hence in the legal institutions of the peoples of that race and explains, for example, why some peoples have bureaucratic administration while others hamper administration by judicially applied checks and balances, why some peoples have codes while others continue to administer justice by means of customary law, and, perhaps, why some peoples have many judges and few lawyers while others have many lawyers and few judges.

[1] *Der Ursprung des Rechts*, 7.
[2] *La vita del diritto*, 2nd ed., Bk 5 (1890).
[3] *L'Idée moderne du droit*, 6th ed., Bk 1, Introduction and chap. 5 (1909), translated in *Modern French Legal Philosophy*, 3–49.
[4] *National Welfare and National Decay* (1921).

As they are applied to the materials of law and of legal history these interpretations are likely to involve a fallacy of looking back at the Middle Ages and the beginnings of modern law in terms of linguistic and political units of today; of seeing a racial unity and racial continuity by looking through the political spectacles of today. Thus it is not uncommon to see Anglo-Norman institutions spoken of as "French" and to read of a "French" element in English law, as there is a French element in English speech. In this respect the ethnological interpretation has shown us a phenomenon which has often been remarked in the history-writing of the last century. For instance, there were theories of Latin and of Germanic civilization, the one leading to unity, the other leading to separation; the one giving us a conception of comprehensive unity in religion and politics and law, the other giving us a conception of individual independence, a negation of unity, in the form of Protestantism, of checks and balances in politics, and of Puritanism in morals. These theories are connected with the economic-ethnological interpretation of modern history that gave rise to what has been called the "epos of the conquered peoples," in which Saxons were set over against Norman conquerors, and Celts or Romans over against Germanic conquerors; the former in each case being taken to be the people which formed the third estate, created the medieval municipalities and in the nineteenth century took over the political as they had already acquired the economic hegemony[1].

One must recognize a core of truth in such interpretations that makes them plausible. It is as mistaken to exclude such factors in legal development as it is to insist upon them as the one or even the main explanation of legal history. Moreover the ethnological interpretation did a special service in leading to recognition of the part which men have played in legal development, even if it did not think in terms of human creative activity. But with all allowances we must pronounce that influence of the race element in determining the course

---

[1] Croce, *Storia della storiografia Italiana nel secolo decimonono*, I, 128. Compare Gooch, *History and Historians in the Nineteenth Century*, 170–172.

of legal development and in shaping legal institutions has been very much exaggerated in every form of ethnological interpretation. They overlook the effect of suggestion and imitation in a subject in which men thought universally from the twelfth to the sixteenth century, and were led to think universally for many purposes by the law-of-nature theory in the seventeenth and eighteenth centuries, and have not wholly ceased to think universally even today in that half of the legal world which has Roman law for the basis of its legal institutions and hence of its legal education. The fact that all lawyers and judges and legislators in Roman-law countries have a common education in the Institutes of Justinian and in modes of professional thought and rules of art deriving from Rome, explains much more in modern law than any exponent of the ethnological interpretation has ever been able to vouch for his theory.

Take, for instance, the argument so often made that codification prevails upon the Continent and in the Latin-American world, but not in English-speaking lands. This argument, when examined, proves too much. No community of race may be vouched to explain why Holland in 1838, Roumania in 1864 and Portugal in 1865 substantially adopted the French civil code, nor may we invoke diversity of race to explain why Portugal enacted a code in 1865 while Brazil did not do so till 1917, so that the two codes are of wholly different types. Nor may we explain in this way why Prussia had a code in 1791, Austria in 1811, and Baden adopted the French code, while Switzerland had none till 1901–1907. Much less shall we understand why the Swiss code became what it is unless we note the course of juristic analysis and systematic ordering of the Roman law under the leadership of the historical jurists of the nineteenth century and the German code of 1900 which was the fruit thereof. Fashions of legislation in the modern world are as independent of race and language as fashions of dress among the upper classes of society. Moreover when we look into the circumstances that have led to codes we see how independent they are of race or nation.

Two classes of countries have adopted codes, countries with well developed legal systems which had exhausted the possibilities of juristic development through the traditional element of their law and required a new basis for a new juristic development, and countries which had their whole legal development before them and required an immediate basis therefor. In such countries four conditions will be found to have existed, which led to codification: (1) the possibilities of juristic development of existing legal materials were exhausted for the time being or there were no such materials at hand since the country had no juristic past; (2) usually the existing law was unwieldy, full of archaisms and uncertain; (3) the growing point of law had shifted to legislation and an efficient organ of legislation had developed; (4) usually there was a need for one law in a political community whose several subdivisions had developed or received divergent local laws. Add to these the Roman tradition, a part of the education of every lawyer except in England and English-settled countries, so that all who had to do with law were brought up on the codification of Justinian, and we may understand why the law of all Roman-law jurisdictions of any importance has been codified. Perhaps we shall perceive also that like conditions may yet lead to codification in the United States, as the continual expansion of uniform state legislation and the partial codifications in our uniform commercial laws abundantly suggest. That the English race is not instinctively averse to codification is shown by the Anglo-Indian codes. Where there was no developed system of courts at hand to receive the law gradually and work out its application to Indian conditions by a process of judicial empiricism, but law and courts had almost to be set up together and hence law had to be set up *en bloc* as a complete system, Englishmen were quite willing to codify.

Again the argument as to centralized bureaucratic administration on the one hand and a system of checks and balances on the other fails when examined critically. The legal and administrative system of republican Rome, with its collegiate magistracies, its co-ordinate jurisdictions, its vetoes and its appeals to the people, hampered administration by legal checks quite as thoroughly as the constitutional system of nineteenth-century America. What we think of as the Roman system is the system of the later empire. What we think of as the historical English system is the system of feudal Europe generally. The conception of the king ruling under God and the law is the conception of the king as a lord of the soil in a relation with his tenants involving reciprocal rights and duties, and proceeds on radically different presuppositions from the constitutional guarantees of natural rights which were formulated in the eighteenth century. Likewise what we think of as the Continental system is the system of the French monarchy of the seventeenth and eighteenth centuries and of eighteenth-century governments on that model. It is significant that territorial expansion, growth of population, commercial and industrial development and economic unification lead toward the latter among all peoples without regard to race or language. The steady march of centralized administration in England, the abandonment in the Arlidge case[1] of Coke's doctrine as to judicial control of administrative methods, and the rise of executive justice by boards and commissions in the United States, speak for themselves[2].

Vico's idea that nations had lives comparable to those of individuals, that their lives ran in an orbit which they were constrained to follow by an unalterable necessity, led to a writing of history founded on the conception of the organic development of peoples. Applied to legal history under the influence of biology, this led presently to biological interpretations. Applied to the doctrine of race spirit or race character as the determining factor in legal development, this type of history-writing led to an interpretation of legal history and of legal institutions as determined by laws of development which in their essence were laws of race development and of race character. Thus three influences combined to give us a positivist comparative ethnological jurisprudence and a positivist ethno-

---

[1] *Local Government Board* v. *Arlidge*, [1915] A.C. 120, [1914] 1 K.B. 160; Dicey, *Law and Public Opinion in England*, 2nd ed. xli–xliv (1914); Dicey, *Law of the Constitution*, 8th ed. xxxvii–xlvii (1915).

[2] Pound, "Executive Justice," 55 *American Law Register*, 137 (1906); Pound, "The Revival of Personal Government," *Proceedings of the New Hampshire Bar Assoc.* 1917, 13; Goodnow, "The Growth of Executive Discretion," *Proceedings of the American Political Science Assoc.* II, 29 (1910); Powell, "Judicial Review of Administrative Action in Immigration Proceedings," 22 *Harvard Law Rev.* 360 (1909).

logical interpretation: the rise of positivism and development of sociology, the quest of the philosophical jurists for a broader basis for philosophy of law, to be found in comparative legal history, folk psychology and ethnology, and the organic version of the existing ethnological interpretation when it was subjected to biological influence. The method was to be a discovery of laws of social and hence of legal development by observation and historical verification. The result was an interpretation in terms of a conflict and harmonizing of instincts—of a conflict between the instinct of individual preservation and the social instinct, between individual self-assertion and social ordering— verified out of comparative legal history and a descriptive sociology which investigated minutely the social institutions of all peoples and particularly those of primitive peoples[1]. For comparative embryology was doing great things about this time in biology, and it was believed that legal institutions in embryo, as it were, would reveal to us the fundamental types and enable us to trace the course of development with assurance.

Post was feeling for something of the first importance when he saw in law an attempt to harmonize instincts in action rather than an attempt to reconcile wills in action. But he could not get away from the ideas in which his generation was brought up nor were sociology and psychology well enough developed to enable him to do what he sought. In effect he put the Kantian reconciliation of the will of each in action with the will of all in terms of instinct and sought to verify it by ethnological

[1] "In fact we see everywhere in social life that on the one side the single biological individual is ruled by individual biological forces directed toward the preservation of his biological individuality and on the other side his individual strivings are diverted and limited by the ordering of the social groups in which he lives. Thus it comes about that every individual is ruled on the one side by egoistic forces, on the other side by moral forces which are unselfish or for the common interest. On the one hand he is himself a mechanical physical system, on the other hand he is part of a mechanical physical system. Thus it comes about also that each biological individual feels himself entitled to rights on the one side and on the other side bound by duties. He feels entitled in his capacity of biological individual; he feels bound in his capacity of member of a social group." Post, *Die Grundlagen des Rechts*, pp. 8–9 (1884).

See also, Post, *Bausteine für einen allgemeinen Rechtswissenschaft* (1880); Post, *Grundriss der Ethnologischen Jurisprudenz* (1894–1895); Post, *Ueber die Aufgaben einer allgemeinen Rechtswissenschaft* (1891).

research instead of demonstrating it by metaphysical speculation or verifying it by history. Also it is easy for us now to see
that he often interpreted primitive social institutions in terms
of problems of modern jurisprudence. In this he did what
lawyers are always prone to do. He did what historical jurists
had done before him in their generalizations of Roman legal
history and what analytical jurists do today when they seek to
apply their universal analyses to the facts of every stage of
Roman law from the *ius strictum* to Justinian and to the facts
of all periods of English law from the thirteenth century to the
present. When a leader of the analytical school tells us that
there are legal conceptions which, if not eternal, are exceedingly
slow of change and "go back as far as we have a clear knowledge
of human affairs and show to our eyes no signs of decay[1]," he
does exactly what Post has been reproached for doing and he
does it for the same reason. To see the nineteenth-century
conception of a legal transaction in liability to restore a thing
certain solemnly delivered, to see nineteenth-century liability
to repair injuries due to culpable conduct in a system of com-
position-penalties, to see the full-blown Roman *dominium* in
legal securing of seisin, is to misrepresent the beginnings of
law quite as much as any positivist ever misrepresented the
beginnings of social control. But the analytical jurist is on
strictly legal ground and has not had to reckon with detection
by modern anthropologists.

What is more serious is that Post wrote in the era of mechanical
sociology, or of the mechanical type of biological sociology,
when it was still held that some one principle was discoverable,
and discoverable by some one sovereign method, whereby we
might arrive at the fundamental laws governing social phenomena. The method and the principle were to be reached through
observation of the phenomena, not determined *à priori* by
metaphysical speculation. But the data were insufficient. Legal
history needed to be re-studied and re-written with the needs
of the social sciences in view. As things were, what seemed
historical evidence was often an interpretation in terms of the
maximum of individual self-assertion as the end of law. The

[1] Gray, *Nature and Sources of the Law,* § 11 (1909).

so-called descriptive sociology was gathering a huge mass of material, most of which was of little or no value for juristic purposes as it stood, but must first be put through the crucible of one of the specialized social sciences. When the jurist sought to utilize such materials, instead of using them to throw light on his special problems he was likely to shape them by his pre-existing legal ideas and thus verify his ideas out of themselves. In short, Durkheim had not yet taught us the limitations and rules of method which are involved in such an undertaking[1]. The positivist ethnological interpretation could be no more than a forerunner of broader and better methods.

Biological interpretation, that is, interpretation in terms of a biological principle of struggle for existence regarded as the law of social and hence of legal development[2], has taken many forms. Often it has been used in connection with other theories, notably in connection with attempts to work out a positivist theory on the basis of the physical environment of the people governed by the body of law under consideration. In general three types may be recognized, the idealistic, the ethnological and the economic. In the idealistic type a biological idea, the struggle for existence or the survival of the fittest, may be taken to be the idea which is realizing in the development of legal institutions. Or, as is more usual, legal history may be conceived as a conflict of ideas, as it were a struggle for existence between legal ideas, and a survival of those which prove fittest to survive through responding best to social needs or social environment. Sometimes the political interpretation is put in biological form and the legal order is interpreted as a well-ordered social struggle for existence among individuals or groups of individuals; as the minimum ordering of this necessary struggle which enables it to go forward most effectively. In another form of this type a conflict of legal institutions is pictured, with survival of the fittest. But the institutions are conceived as expressions of ideas, so that ultimately the conflict is one of ideas. Perhaps the best of this type is Richard's inter-

[1] *Les règles de la méthode sociologique*, 6th ed. (1912).
[2] Neukamp, *Entwickelungsgeschichte des Rechts* (1895); Kuhlenbeck, *Natürliche Grundlagen des Rechts* (1905); Seitz, *Biologie des geschichtlich positiven Rechts* (1906–1910).

pretation in terms of a conflict of social with anti-social rules
and institutions and doctrines, that is, of those which further
the existence of the social group with those which interfere
therewith or hamper its functioning and development[1].

In recent positivist theories of law the biological phraseology
and the idealistic cast are discarded and we are told, in what is
substantially the same interpretation, that "to act in conformity
with right and law is to act in conformity to what is social,"
that "the jural principle (*la règle de droit*) says: do such a thing
because it is social; refrain from doing such and such a thing
because it is anti-social." The author quoted from adds: "A
juridical obligation is...an obligation to do what has a social
value, that is, not to do what is anti-social....The criterion of
the jural principle is the social reaction which is caused by the
violation of the principle; a reaction that is capable of being
socially organized. Let us not say," he goes on, "that the jural
principle cannot be founded on a fact, since it is nothing more
than a precept to conform oneself to facts[2]." If he is speaking
here of law as a whole, one may assent, for the existence of
civilized society calls for peace and order and the legal order is
in large part a response to that demand. But the question is not
merely one of the social value of law in the abstract but of legal
institutions and rules and doctrines, in short, of laws as we find
them. How does the obligation resting on the individual man
to do what has a social value and not to do what is anti-social
help us when we must determine whether or not to apply the
Rule in Shelley's Case or the doctrine of merger of contingent
remainders, as courts have had to do in more than one American
state in recent years? Without much more detail as to social
values and as to what is anti-social, we have no help from such
a formula. If we seek to use it, one will fill the content of "social
value" with the idea of a maximum of individual self-assertion,
in which he had been trained, and another with ideas of
securing a minimum human existence to each individual, and
another with something else. Duguit would fill it out with
promoting social interdependence through division of labour,

---

[1] *L'Origine de l'idée de droit* (1892).
[2] Duguit, *Les transformations générales du droit privé*, 24–29 (1912).

that is, with an idea of the maximum of productive efficiency of an industrial society crowded in a limited area. If the jurist must wait until agreement is reached as to the ultimate and supreme social value before he can have a philosophical criterion, or must work with a criterion which each may fill out for himself in this way, it is not unlikely that we may have for a time a reversion to a personal—one might say an oriental—administration of justice.

Is it not possible that there are social values and that we may think of conserving or furthering them so far as we may and with least sacrifice of them as a whole, even if we cannot agree on the one single ultimate social value? May we expect to weigh all the demands and desires of men in society with one weight? Economic claims, moral and religious claims, cultural claims, the claims of the individual spiritual life—may we expect to unify these for juristic purposes and say that all things legal shall be judged by the common denominator? May not an act run counter to one social value and yet further another and is it not precisely this circumstance which gives difficulty in such cases as freedom of the press and free speech, where we have on the one side a social interest in the security of social institutions and on the other a social interest in general progress, of which free individual thinking and speaking and writing have always been a prime agency[1]? What seems anti-social from one standpoint does not seem anti-social from another. If it is meant that the test is what is anti-social in the result, that is, what is anti-social after weighing these interests against one another or after seeing how far they are infringed respectively and how a compromise may be made, the formula is of little use. The "simple question" put is too simple. So also as to the "precept to conform oneself to facts." What Duguit means is that the picture before us in developing and applying legal materials shall be an exact design of social interdependence through division of labour, a verifiable phenomenon, not some speculative plan. But which shall we say conforms to this exact blue-print plan, merger of contingent remainders or the reverse? Are

---

[1] See Chafee, *Freedom of Speech* (1920); *Liberty of Speech, Papers and Proceedings, American Sociological Society*, vol. 9 (1914).

not some other and vital "facts" of social existence involved
in a statute imposing penalties upon certain publications, to be
judged with reference to constitutional guarantees of free speech,
over and above the interdependence through division of labour
that is so conspicuous in a modern industrial society? And if
these are referred to "interdependence through similarity of
interest," in that we are all human beings, which is to give way
or how are they to be reconciled or compromised? In truth, as
Croce has observed, these positivist interpretations are apt at
bottom to be Hegelian. The idea of freedom is replaced by an
idea of "the social." The inexorable law is not progressive
unfolding of freedom as an idea; it is progressive unfolding of
"the social" by organization of the social reaction against the
anti-social.

Ethnological forms of the biological interpretation picture a
conflict of race institutions with survival of the fittest. Enough
has been said of such theories in connection with the ethnological
interpretation as such.

An economic form was urged by Vaccaro[1], who took legal
institutions and rules and doctrines to be the results of a class
conflict, or series of class conflicts, determined by survival of
the socially fittest. Expressing the needs or desires of the class
which was dominant socially or politically for the time being,
they came into conflict with rival institutions or rules or doctrines expressing the needs or desires of other classes. Thus
what in political and economic history is class conflict, in legal
history is a conflict of institutions and ideas. As it is easy to
see that Gumplowicz's interpretation in terms of race conflict[2]
is a rationalization of the existing situation in late nineteenth-
century Austria, put universally, so it is not hard to see that
Vaccaro's class conflict is a rationalization of the industrial and
agrarian agitation in Italy, put universally. As we shall see
when we come to the economic interpretation, there is a kernel
of truth in Vaccaro's theory that gives it a certain plausibility.
But when we try it upon the difficult problems of legal science—

[1] Vaccaro, *Les bases sociologiques de droit et de l'état* (1898), transl. of
Le basi del diritto e dello stato (1893). See also Bentley, *The Process of
Government*, 287 (1908).
[2] *Der Rassenkampf* (1883).

the problem of rule or discretion, of application of law, of juridical method—or when we try it upon particular problems, such as freedom of contract or freedom of speech, or the clash of interests involved in present-day industrial disputes, we shall find that it leaves the most significant phenomena of the traditional legal materials unexplained and does nothing for us to help us handle those materials, unless it is implied that we may hope to do no more than follow Mr Pickwick's maxim and shout with the larger mob. Indeed attempt to interpret the rules of English law with respect to border trees and the vacillation of courts between the principle of seisin and the Roman-law solution, borrowed from Greek philosophy, of asking where the tree took root[1]; or to interpret the conflict between the same principle of seisin and the Roman conception of gift as a legal transaction dependent on intent, which made it uncertain down to 1890 whether delivery was required in a gift of chattels *inter vivos*[2]; or to understand the anomalous doctrine as to

[1] In Roman law if a tree set in the land of Titius takes root in the land of Maevius it belongs to Maevius; if it takes root in the land of each it is common property. *Inst.* 2, 1, 31. Bracton lays down the Roman rule in the words of the Institutes, 1569 ed., fol. 10. In *Masters* v. *Pollie*, 2 Rolle, 141 (1620), it was held that in such a case the tree belongs to the owner of the land in which it was planted because "the main part of the tree being in the soil of the plaintiff, the residue of the tree belongs to him also." In *Waterman* v. *Soper*, 1 Ld. Raym. 737 (1697–8), Lord Holt, apparently in ignorance of the prior decision, ruled that "if *A* plants a tree upon the extremest limit of his land and the tree growing extend its root into the land of *B* next adjoining, *A* and *B* are tenants in common of this tree." The reasoning is that of the Institutes: "And therefore a tree planted near a boundary, if it stretch out its roots into the neighbour's ground also, becomes common property." *Inst.* 2, 1, 31. In *Holder* v. *Coates*, Moody & M. 112 (1827), Littledale, J., when confronted with this conflict in the authorities, chose the rule of *Masters* v. *Pollie*.

The Roman rule is taken from the Greek philosophical doctrine of form and substance and Aristotle's theory of the composition of plants. *Hist. Animal.* v, 1, *Meteorol.* iv, 8; Sokolowski, *Philosophie im Privatrecht*, i, 148 ff. Compare the reasoning in *Dig.* 29, 2, 9, § 2 and 41, 1, 26, § 1. The rule announced by the King's Bench in 1620, which finally prevailed, goes on the idea of seisin. Titius planted the tree and is seised of the trunk, which is the main thing, no matter where the roots may stray.

I have discussed these cases more fully in "Juristic Science and Law," 31 *Harvard Law Rev.* 1047, 1050–1053 (1918).

[2] *Inst.* 2, 7, § 2; French Civil Code, art. 938; Baudry-Lacantinerie, *Précis de droit civil*, 11th ed. iii, §§ 803–808; Schuster, *Principles of German Civil Law*, §§ 199–200; Dernburg, *Pandekten*, 8th ed. ii, § 363, note 2. As to the common law, see notes 2–5, ante p. 50. I have discussed this subject at large in "Juristic Science and Law," 31 *Harvard Law Rev.* 1047, 1053–1058.

impossible and illegal conditions in testamentary gifts, given a further analogical development in French law, abolished by many recent codes, and borrowed by English equity for testamentary gifts of chattels while the general rule for other legal transactions applies to devises of land[1]—attempt to explain such things, which are the staple of legal phenomena, by a principle of class conflict or as resulting from "action and reaction of men" or of human desires beyond the lawyer's desire for logical consistency or his desire to cleave to authority or his desire to find a principle of reason in which he could rest, is palpably futile.

Taken as a whole, the various interpretations we have been considering have three features that account sufficiently for their failure to maintain themselves. They assume that one single principle will sufficiently explain all legal phenomena. They exclude creative activity and look upon law as something we may only observe in order to verify hypotheses as to the principles of its development; as something beyond juristic power to shape except as the unconscious instrument of inexorable forces. They consider and seek to account for a limited portion of the whole mass of legal phenomena, leaving traditional modes of thought and rules of art and the psychology of authority and of imitation quite out of account. Nor are they written around any such cores of truth as made the ethical and political interpretations so much nearer to reality. In truth these ethnological and biological interpretations have little for us beyond two analogies, the analogy of the principles of mechanical physics and the analogy of an organism. The former fails because social phenomena are phenomena of life. The other and more plausible analogy fails in that an organism is adapting itself to environment, or at least is being acted on and shaped immediately by the pressure of the environment. Law, on the other hand, is fashioned from without to meet human needs and wants and desires. True these may arise out of the environment. But law is not adapting itself by its internal power of response to stimulus nor is it subject to immediate and direct

[1] See Pound, "Legacies on Impossible and Illegal Conditions Precedent," 3 *Illinois Law Rev.* 1 (1908).

pressure from the outward circumstances of the life to which it is to be applied.

And yet these interpretations have done something for the science of law as it is today. They have led us to a wider basis for philosophy of law. They have introduced thorough study of primitive social and legal institutions and thus have exploded many traditional false ideas that had come down from the days of the state-of-nature theory. They have given added impetus to the movement for unification of the social sciences by establishing connections with ethnology and anthropology and social psychology. Most of all they have suggested lines of preparatory work that must be carried on before we may achieve an adequate social theory and hence an adequate theory of law as a social phenomenon.

V

THE ECONOMIC INTERPRETATION

In its last phase the search for a single supreme cause of all
legal phenomena turned from ethnology and biology to economics, a direction in which several philosophical paths at length
converged. One of these paths was idealism, leading to what
has been called historical materialism. Another was positivism,
through endeavour to discover economic laws by observation
of social and legal phenomena. Still another was realism,
through the so-called economic realism. The hegemony of the
natural sciences in the nineteenth century and consequent
naturalistic conception of the world led to increased attention
to men's physical surroundings, material wants and physical
activities to satisfy those wants. Likewise the problem of the
time had ceased to be political in form, as in the fore part of the
nineteenth century, and had taken on an economic form. The
question of reconciling political freedom with authority, which
had been agitated for a century, was superseding by the so-
called social question, consequent upon change from an agri-
cultural-commercial to an industrial economy and the rise of
the industrial labourers as a class-conscious group of political
importance urging demands under conditions for which the
traditional legal order made scant provision. Thus a shifting
from the political standpoint to the economic standpoint grew
out of new conditions with which the social sciences had to
deal and of new phenomena which they were required to
explain.

As is well known, economic interpretation[1] began in the fifth
decade of the nineteenth century when Marx applied the
Hegelian dialectic to English political economy, to the theories

[1] On the economic interpretation generally, see Seligman, *The Economic
Interpretation of History*, 2nd ed.; Croce, *Materialismo storico ed economia
marxista*, 4th ed., translated as *Historical Materialism and the Economics of Karl
Marx*. For the economic interpretation in jurisprudence, see Leist, *Privatrecht und Kapitalismus im neunzehnten Jahrhundert* (1911).

of French historians of the French Revolution and to his own experience of the proletarian movement. These materials were given shape by a material idea, if one may put it so, and thus treated suggested a new way of understanding history. At first it was but suggested. In 1859 it was formulated in what became an oft-quoted passage[1], but it attracted little notice for a generation. In 1885 it began to be urged and it sprang into full bloom about 1890. It had great vogue in Germany and in Italy in the last decade of the nineteenth century, when it came to be applied to every form of history, and it got no less vogue in America in the decade from 1900 to 1910, the era of Rooseveltian progressivism. In that decade it passed over into Anglo-American juristic thought and it is still a force to be reckoned with in jurisprudence, especially in America.

Considered as a general theory of social institutions and of history, the economic interpretation had two elements. On the one hand there was an older, metaphysical element. For the economic interpretation in all its forms proceeds on a conception of reality over against appearance, of substance as contrasted with accident. It postulates a sort of historical god pulling the threads that cause the puppet actors to move this way or that and so produce the appearance which we call history. Prior thinkers had merely misconceived this god. He was not the "idea" or the "absolute" or the "unconscious." He was economic. But the conception of history was the same. It was something moving in a fixed orbit according to a fore-ordained plan toward an ultimate state of perfection. This terminal state was not ethical (right) nor political (freedom). It was not biological (the social organism perfectly adapted to its surroundings). It was economic—a condition of maximum satisfaction of material wants. On the other hand there was a newer element in the doctrine, namely, the concrete economic idea; the dialectic of the concrete needs or wants of men in place of the abstract dialectic of freedom. The former element brought into the economic interpretation the tendency to construct history à priori and to ignore facts as not significant, which is so marked in all idealistic interpretations and their

[1] *Zur Kritik der politischen Oekonomie*, IV, V (1859).

derivatives. The other element, however, tended to correct this and to compel a fresh examination of all the evidence, including much which had been ignored, in an endeavour to find economic laws[1].

An evolutionary version of the Marxian idealistic economic interpretation gave rise to a positivist form which is its second stage. This begins with Engels' book on the origin of the family, of private property and of the state, in 1884. It was carried to an extreme in the next decade and is represented in an economic ethnological interpretation of legal history mentioned already in another connection. It was applied to the history of the law of property by Loria one of whose books was translated into English and exerted some influence in America[2]. He conceived of all history in terms of an economic struggle for control of land and of social evolution as involving successive stages of slavery, serfdom and payment of rent, leading to an ultimate freedom of the soil by means of small proprietorships. It was applied to criminal law by positivist criminologists[3], who sought a philosophy of legal history in terms of economic evolution. Also a special form arose in America from the grafting of a mechanical-positivist economic interpretation on the orthodox English analytical jurisprudence. Thus we may recognize three types of economic interpretation of law and of legal history: the idealistic form, in which they are interpreted in terms of the unfolding of an economic idea; the mechanical-sociological type, which identifies social laws with economic laws and seeks to work out a social mechanics and a social physics on economic lines; and the mechanical analytical type which, accepting the analytical dogma that law is the command of the sovereign, conceives of the sovereign as a mere mouthpiece through which economically determined social forces make themselves heard. Perhaps one should add that while socialists have commonly urged the first and second types, there is no necessary connection

[1] I owe this account of the subject to Croce, *Storia della storiografia Italiana nel secolo decimonono*, II, 219–221.

[2] *La teoria economica della costituzione politica* (1886); *Le basi economiche della costituzione sociale* (1902), translated by Keasbey as *The Economic Foundations of Society* (1907).

[3] In a way this goes back to Godwin, *Political Justice*, 15–16, 455–458 (1796).

between any of them and communist socialism or, indeed, any socialism. The third has been urged by some American teachers of law who are staunch upholders of the traditional common law and of the social order which it postulates.

We need pause but a moment over the idealistic type. In place of the ethical idea (right) or the political idea (freedom) or the ethnological idea (race spirit or race character) or the biological idea (natural selection) it put an economic idea—an idea of the satisfaction of material wants. Thus, as Croce aptly puts it, the idealistic economic interpretation was the "Hegelian left[1]." History was interpreted not in terms of man's ethical life as a moral entity, nor in terms of his political life as a political animal, but in terms of his economic life. History was the march in the world of an idea of economic activity to satisfy man's economic wants. Hence all legal history was economic. It was a "history of wants and of labour[2]." Obviously all that has been said of the method of the idealistic interpretations of legal history applies here also. We are not required to choose one of them. At most the question for us today is as to the relative size of the core of truth which we must concede to each. As that core, whatever it may be, is common to all forms of the economic interpretation, we may defer looking at it until the other types have been characterized more fully.

Only a matter of emphasis distinguishes the mechanical or positivist sociological type from the economic phase of the ethnological interpretation. Indeed this type commonly runs into or is developed in connection with some form of ethnological or biological interpretation. Its distinguishing mark is reliance on the analogies of physics rather than on those of biology and a thinking of race character in terms of economic environment and economic development rather than psychologically. Thus we are told by an exponent of this doctrine that "law is a resultant of forces which arise from the struggle for existence among men." "It is," he adds, "the will of a sovereign precisely in the sense that the earth's orbit, which is the resultant of a

---

[1] *The Philosophy of Hegel*, 201–202; *Storia della storiografia Italiana nel secolo decimonono*, II, 218.

[2] Croce, *Riduzione della filosofia del diritto alla filosofia dell' economia* (1907).

conflict between centrifugal and centripetal force, is the will of a sovereign. Both the law and the orbit are necessities[1]." Neither, he says elsewhere, has any relation to an idea of right and justice[2]. The earth's orbit is an inevitable product of physical forces; the law is an inevitable product of economic forces. The mode of thought here is familiar. All that is new is the name and dress of the relentless ultimate cause which the jurist may recognize but may not swerve from its course. Nothing, says Hegel, has power against the march of the spirit. In contrast with the absolute power of the people whose natural principle represents a stage in the self-developing world spirit, "the spirits of other peoples are void of power[3]." "What you have as a scientific fact," says an American exponent of the economic interpretation, "is an automatic conflict of forces reaching along the paths of least resistance a result favourable to the dominant energy[4]." "The law being," he says elsewhere, "the resultant of the forces in conflict, must ultimately be deflected in the direction of the stronger and be used to crown the victor[5]." In Hegel's words, nothing has power against the march of the economic law. In contrast with the absolute power of the class whose social dominance represents a stage in the self-developing economic law, the self-interest of other classes is void of effect. And yet those who spoke thus affected to have dispensed with philosophy and to have outgrown metaphysics as a mere stage in the inexorable course of development of human thought.

Much of the evidence upon which the adherents of the economic interpretation have relied was drawn from legislation. Hence the dogma of the historical school, that law might be found but not made, was less adapted to their conception than the dogma of the analytical school that law was the command of the sovereign, or, in its later form, a body of rules recognized and enforced by the judicial organs of the sovereign. The part of the law which appeared significant from the standpoint of their interpretation was not the traditional modes of thought

[1] Brooks Adams in *Centralization and the Law*, 23 (1906).
[2] *Id.* 35.   [3] *Grundlinien der Philosophie des Rechts*, § 347.
[4] Brooks Adams in *Centralization and the Law*, 35.
[5] *Id.* 133.

and rules of art but particular precepts for conduct, enacted or judicially applied, which might be traced to the self-interest of an economically and hence socially dominant class, making itself felt through pressure upon legislator or judge and giving rise to or moulding statute or judicial pronouncement. They might agree with the historical jurist that these formulations as such were relatively unimportant; that they were but appearance and that reality was in the background. But they could not admit that the reality in the background was something, already law, which was there waiting to be discovered and formulated. To them the reality was something that operated upon law-maker and judge and dictated their utterances, not something for which they were searching and from time to time were able partially to uncover. "The Sovereign being only a vent or mouthpiece," says Brooks Adams, "the form the mouthpiece takes or the name given to it is immaterial[1]." The political interpretation and institutional legal history interpret illusion. "The dominant class...will shape the law to favour themselves and that code will most nearly approach the ideal of justice of each particular age which favours most perfectly the dominant class[2]." That is, the ethical interpretation and doctrinal legal history also interpret illusion. "The law has been molded by ...the self interest of successive dominant classes...as they have risen to power. These dominant classes have named the judges who...have made and interpreted precedents. They also have controlled legislatures and have passed statutes to effect their purpose when the courts could not do their bidding[3]."

It will be seen that Brooks Adams puts economic determinism behind English analytical jurisprudence. Law is made by a sovereign or is recognized and applied by the organs of a sovereign. But in so making or recognizing or applying it they but register the self-interest of the dominant class as it is inevitably determined by economic laws. For purposes of

[1] *Id.* 63.
[2] *Id.* 63–64. "Upon conditions that the ruling class finds profitable to its aims and advantageous to its power, are built codes of morality as well as of law, which codes are but reflections of those all-potent class interests." Myers, *History of the Supreme Court of the United States*, 8.
[3] Brooks Adams, "The Modern Conception of Animus," 19 *Green Bag*, 12, 17 (1907).

formal juristic analysis we speak of a sovereign. When we look deeper we must speak of an economic conflict. Where Austin pictures a sovereign issuing commands on the basis of utility, Brooks Adams would have us see a dominant class issuing commands, through the mask of the legal order, on the basis of its self-interest. Benthamist utilitarianism has been replaced by mechanical positivism. The ethical element latent in Austin has been wholly excluded. There is no need of Bentham's science of legislation whereby the sovereign may know how to command what utility requires. The socially and economically strongest will get their own way and juristic science can do no more than observe this law and verify its workings in the phenomena of administration of justice.

In this respect the economic interpretation carries to an extreme the separation and exclusion of the ethical element in juristic thought which began in analytical jurisprudence with Bentham as a reaction from Blackstone and in the historical school with Savigny as a reaction from the identification of law and morals in the philosophical jurisprudence of the seventeenth and eighteenth centuries. Austin's successors have urged that he made a great advance upon Bentham in that, whereas Bentham classified the science of legislation under jurisprudence, Austin showed that jurisprudence had nothing to do with ethics and hence nothing to do with legislation—that Austin had first grasped decisively the distinction between law and morals[1]. These writers also were protesting against the identification of law and morals, with its implication that moral validity is the criterion of the legal obligation of positive law, as it survived in legal institutional text-books in the nineteenth century. Austin studied at Bonn under Mackeldey[2] and thus came in contact with Kant's rejection of the identification and Kant's conception that instead of eternal precepts of actual law there were but eternal principles of making law by which the actual precepts might be criticized. In the collection of books which Austin left at his death[3] the significant institutional treatises

[1] E.g. Markby, *Elements of Law*, 4th ed., § 12 (1889).
[2] See Mrs Austin's sketch in Austin, *Jurisprudence*, 4th ed., I, 5–6.
[3] Austin, *Jurisprudence*, 4th ed., I, ix–x.

are Mackeldey and Hugo; and Kant's writings on the philosophy of law and morals are included. The edition of Hugo's *Encyklopädie* which he used[1] is purely Kantian on this subject and in the edition of Mackeldey which he used (for later editions are tinctured with the ideas of the historical school) the distinction between natural law and positive law is stated in Kantian terms[2]. Thus we might expect that Austin's views as to the relation between law and morals would be much influenced by Kant. In fact they are Kant grafted on Bentham. Each of the two elements of Brooks Adams' doctrine is indifferent to ethics.

Historical jurists developed the reaction from the identification of law and morals in one direction by a doctrine which at least implies that the science of legislation is unnecessary. Austin developed it in another direction by a rigid separation of jurisprudence from ethics. The law as given was to be studied analytically and the function of the jurist and province of jurisprudence went no further. Yet Austin conceded that there was a science of legislation, resting upon utilitarian ethics. The positivists, taking the position of the historical school, though for other reasons, eliminated the science of legislation and its ethical foundation. On the one hand they were attacking the "supernatural" as something intervening in the course of natural phenomena. On the other hand they were attacking the idea of "chance" and insisting that all phenomena but manifested the regular and orderly workings of exact laws. Ethics was under suspicion because of its possible relations to the one bogie. Legislation in Coke's sense was under suspicion because of the relation of a theory of parliamentary omnipotence and sovereign will to the other bogie. Coming to their mechanical-positivist jurisprudence some from the analytical school and some from the historical school, the American adherents of the economic interpretation carried forward the two sides of the reaction against identification of law and morals to their conclusion. In his zeal against ideas of right and justice and confusion of law and morals, Brooks Adams but goes a bit

[1] 7th ed. (1823), p. 9.
[2] *Lehrbuch des römischen Rechts*, 7th ed., § 2 (1827).

further than Markby along the same path and in his casting out the science of legislation he but goes to the end of the path laid down in Maine's *Early History of Institutions*[1].

When we turn to the proofs adduced in support of the economic interpretation, we shall find that usually the chief reliance is upon penal legislation of little permanence and relatively little effectiveness in the actual ordering of society or the every-day administration of justice. It is an interpretation of the least enduring and least effective materials of the legal order. But some American adherents of the doctrine have sought to establish it by examination of the doctrinal and institutional history of the common law and their arguments must be looked into more in detail. Brooks Adams vouches the history of the common-law writs from the Norman kings to the Statute of Westminster II and judicial interpretation thereof[2], the history of the rise of the Court of Chancery[3] and the rise of the nineteenth-century doctrine of liability as the corollary of culpability[4]. Professor Bohlen has interpreted the doctrine of *Rylands* v. *Fletcher* and its history in America with much ability and ingenuity in terms of economics[5]. Professor Wyman has suggested a like interpretation of the development of a law of public utilities[6]. President Wilson interpreted the common-law as to injuries by the fault of a fellow servant and assumption of risk along the same lines[7]. Let us consider some of these and ask ourselves how far the case has been made.

As Brooks Adams sees the history of the common-law writs, the king at first, when he wanted a writ for any special purpose, "ordered one to his liking...and a clerk in chancery wrote it." Presently this making of writs to order, as it were, became a potential source of revenue and the barons objected because

---

[1] Maine, *Early History of Institutions*, Lecture 12 (1874), 4th ed., 344–345.

[2] *Centralization and the Law*, 31–35.

[3] *Ibid.*

[4] "The Modern Conception of Animus," 19 *Green Bag*, 12.

[5] The Rule in *Rylands* v. *Fletcher*, 59 *University of Pennsylvania Law Rev.* 298 (1911).

[6] *Public Service Companies*, I, §§ 1–14 (1911). See also Wyman, *The Control of the Market*, I (1911).

[7] *The New Freedom*, 14–15 (1916).

"if justice could be sold to the highest bidder, their days were numbered." Hence they exacted a promise from John that he would not sell justice and later insisted that the chancellor should sell no new writs but should adhere to ancient usage. But the volume of business in the king's courts became such that the king's business could not be done with the existing writs and parliament undertook to provide a remedy through the Statute of Westminster II. The landed gentry were too strong for the king. The judges fell "under the influence of the great magnates of the time, as judges will," and the statute achieved little[1].

You will have perceived that the argument is based on Coke's and Blackstone's version of the Statute of Westminster II and the judicial interpretation thereof. Much of it must fall if that version fails. Nor does it take account of related phenomena which must be reckoned with in any interpretation. Down to the thirteenth century we are at most in a stage of transition to the strict law. Hence law is fluid and at times much depends upon the wilful personality of the king. But Henry II was by instinct a lawyer and Glanvill's book, based on writs, shows that in the twelfth century the lawyer was at work upon them, seeking to put system into them and to make a strict law out of a mass of legal materials that had developed more or less hap-hazard. In other words, a conscious endeavour for something not dependent on will and resistant to class interest and class influence must be recognized. Also we must remember the medieval conception of law as an immemorial custom and that the king was bound by the law. Nor may we forget that aristocracies have always stood firmest for individual liberty because, it may be, the aristocrat, in the heyday of an aristocracy, is apt to have a vigorous personality and to think in terms of individual self-assertion. Accordingly if we compare the provisions of Magna Carta with the statutory special privileges of soldiers under the Roman empire, we shall see a significant difference. In the former concrete propositions are put as universal rules of general application. In the latter there are no more than arbitrary special rules. It is no wonder that the

---

[1] *Centralization and the Law*, 31–35.

one left its mark on the public law of the modern world while the other proved transient. The Middle Ages thought of justice and right in fixed theological terms and conceived them as above and beyond all action of sovereigns. Such ideas coloured and gave direction to special movements that may have had economic origins. The ethical interpretation sees only the former; the economic interpretation sees only the latter. If we must choose, the ethical interpretation often has more for us.

But the argument breaks down in any event in its version of the Statute of Westminster II[1]. The legal order was entering on a stage of strict law. Men were fearful of latitude in procedure. If English law was to be systematized and developed logically, as men saw had happened with the Roman law, the issuance of writs must be reduced to a system. Accordingly lawyers sought to cut down the wide discretion of chancery in this respect and the judges were carrying out the spirit of the statute when they understood it as they did. Blackstone looked back at it through eighteenth-century spectacles and saw a modern problem of unshackling procedure where the problem of the thirteenth century was to tie it down.

Again, take the argument from the rise of the Court of Chancery. We are told that in the class contest, which took the outward form of a contest between the king and the barons, when it had proved impossible to liberalize the law through the common-law courts, the king turned to his council and began to deal with causes directly through the council or committees thereof, thus giving rise to a new type of courts. The most effective weapon developed by this type of tribunal was the writ of subpoena. So "whenever the gentry could control the House of Commons they petitioned against the prerogative courts and clamoured for a return to the common law." But the process went on. "Thus," we are told, "the Chancellor... became ultimately the vent through which the energy of the growing power of capital found expression[2]." It may occur to you to ask why the Chancellor should have relieved against

[1] See Maitland, *Equity and the Forms of Action at Common Law*, 345–346.
[2] *Centralization and the Law*, 34.

penal bonds and allowed redemption of mortgaged property, if his jurisdiction was the expression of the self-interest of the moneyed class as against the strict law which represented the self-interest of the land owners. For the latter were borrowers, not lenders. Also it may be asked whether the break-down of ecclesiastical jurisdiction which had divided the field of administration of justice not unequally with the king's courts should not be put in the scale. Which was most active in limiting and then breaking down this jurisdiction, the feudal aristocracy or the rising moneyed class of the towns?

In truth we cannot tell such complicated stories in such simple fashion. When we seek to explain the opposition of the commons to the court of chancery in the fifteenth and sixteenth centuries we must note some analogous phenomena. Not to go outside of Anglo-American law, we must compare the opposition of the Commonwealth, which certainly did not represent the feudal aristocracy, to equity, which it sought to abolish[1], the opposition of the Puritan to equity in America[2] and Jefferson's opposition to a later liberalizing of the law through what he called "Mansfield's innovations[3]." Three factors in such phenomena are not to be ignored. In the first place new institutions were involved which men did not understand and of which in consequence they were suspicious. Apart from solicitude for stability and the general security, there is a special reason for this in the case of lawyers which more than once has led them to stand out for traditional methods and rules of art against every sort of pressure. They are not willing to give up a technique which they know thoroughly for a new one of which they have had no experience, and easily find arguments against doing so. Secondly, men were rightly jealous of wide magisterial discretion. There was no system of equity. There were no settled principles governing the exercise of discretion, as there are today. Hence lawyers might well feel about extensions of equitable jurisdiction

[1] Parkes, *History of the Court of Chancery*, chap. 8.
[2] See *Quincy's Reports* (Massachusetts), 538 ff. As to other colonies, see Fisher, "Equity in Pennsylvania," *Select Essays in Anglo-American Legal History*, II, 810; Wilson, "Chancery in the Colonies," *id.* 779.
[3] Letter of Jefferson to John Tyler; Tyler, *Letters and Times of the Tylers*, I, 35.

as they do today about the large summary powers we are confiding to administrative boards and commissions[1]. Third, all discretion ran counter to Puritan religious ideas, no matter what the social or economic position of the particular Puritan. Men were to be with one another not over one another. There was to be a government of laws and not of men[2]. The individual conscience was to be guided and persuaded by good laws, made in advance, giving light to the individual at the crisis of action, not coerced by administrative tribunals acting according to the notions of those who sat therein as to what equity and good conscience might require in a particular situation. These things are not to be explained merely in terms of the self-interest of social classes in England in the sixteenth and seventeenth centuries.

In its beginnings the common law, like the Roman law in the same stage of development, imposed liability upon one simply because he or that which he protected had acted and the action had brought about injury. In the seventeenth century we see signs of a change, and in the nineteenth century it was an accepted juristic doctrine that one is liable not for causation as such but for culpable causation and that the culpable mind is the decisive element. This development also has been vouched as establishing the economic interpretation in terms of class interest[3]. But those who so argue must explain much more than they have taken into account in their argument. For the development of a theory of liability is but an item in a series of closely related changes in which the strict law was made over by ideas of equity and natural law and later the legal system crystallized and became rigid once more in what may be called the maturity of the common law. Responsibility for culpable causation, superseding liability for all causation of injury, is but a part of the movement from the legal person as the legal unit to the human being as a moral unit and hence a legal unit; from form to substance; from regard only to the outward to regard chiefly for the inward; from rules to principles and standards; from

[1] E.g. the "Replication of a Serjeant at Law" to Doctor and Student, Hargrave, *Law Tracts*, 325.
[2] *Massachusetts Bill of Rights*, § 30 (1780).
[3] See note 4, ante p. 100.

mechanical application to reasoned individualized application; from authority *qua* authority to authority resting upon reason and justice; and of the later counter-movement to organize and systematize the elements taken into the law during the former process. The moral unit was morally responsible for culpable conduct. Hence the legal unit, identified with the moral unit, should be liable on the same basis. Such was the creative idea. There must be a universal principle of liability by which all cases might be measured and upon which all rules might be strung, and this principle was responsibility for culpable causation. Such was the organizing and systematizing idea of the nineteenth century. Exactly the same process of absorption of moral conceptions and putting them to creative use, followed by a making them over into principles of organization and systematization, may be seen in the Roman law in the transition from the strict law to the juristic law under the influence of natural law in the earlier empire and thence to the maturity of legal system from Diocletian to Justinian. It may be seen in Continental Europe in the transition from the Commentators to the law-of-nature school and thence to the codified law of the nineteenth century. No doubt these things go along with movements of civilization and the economic changes involved therein. But before one may interpret particular items thereof in terms of class conflict and self-interest of the dominant class in society in a particular time and place, he must look into the relation of those items to the development of the whole body of the law as well as analogous phenomena in other systems in like stages of legal development, although as like as not under quite distinct social and economic conditions and with distinct problems of class conflict.

A more sober argument, more critically carried out and with more truth behind it, may be seen in Professor Bohlen's exposition of *Rylands* v. *Fletcher* and the refusal of American courts a generation ago to receive the doctrine of that case as a part of the common law. He says rightly that liability without regard to fault for things done or maintained upon land will appeal differently to judges in a highly organized society whose natural resources have been fully developed than to judges in a pioneer country whose natural resources are under exploitation. In the former courts will be likely to think in terms of preserving existing wealth. In the latter they will think in terms of "permutation of opportunity into wealth[1]." This is sound and might be generalized by saying that in the endeavour of courts to decide upon principles of reason, they draw an ideal picture of the social order with which they are familiar and find therein the designs of reason which they take to be the plan of the law. But the argument proceeds in a way that is more doubtful. In England, we are told, the landed gentry were the dominant class, and the judges, drawn therefrom or associating therewith or hoping to establish themselves or their families therein, reflected the opinions of that class. "To such a class," we are told, "it is inevitable that the right of exclusive dominion over land should appear paramount to its commercial utilization—to them commerce and manufacture, in which they had little or no direct interest, appeared comparatively unimportant." On the other hand, it is said, America was settled for the most part by the commercial and artisan classes. It is said that the whole Puritan movement was a revolt against the social and political conceptions of the landed aristocracy, and that inbred class instinct led the American farmer, himself a land owner, not to attach the same sanctity to proprietary rights as were attached to them by a caste which for generations had lived and governed and thought not so much as men as in the capacity of land owners. Hence while to English judges "land is primarily a private domain, an estate from which the owner derives his power and dignity, within which he must be supreme and undisturbed by intrusions," to American judges "land is a possession, an asset to be utilized for the economic advantages of the possessor[2]."

There can be no question of the ingenuity of this account of *Rylands* v. *Fletcher* on the one hand and, let us say, the rejection of the doctrine by the courts of Pennsylvania on the other hand. But let us consider a few points in more detail. You know better

---

[1] "The Rule in *Rylands* v. *Fletcher*," 59 *University of Pennsylvania Law Rev.* 298, 318.

[2] *Id.* 318–320.

than I whether Sir Leicester Deadlock or Mr Podsnap or
Josiah Bounderby of Coketown is to be taken as standing for
the dominant class in England in 1867. However that may be,
a judge who played the leading part in the final judgment in
Rylands v. *Fletcher* rose to notice at the bar as a commercial
lawyer and one must pause before asserting of him that commerce and manufacture were unimportant in his eyes. Nor may
we say in other connections that American judges have attached
less sanctity to the proprietary rights of land owners than English
judges, or have inclined to deviate from the policies of English
law in which land is assumed to be a permanent acquisition,
held for enduring purposes, while chattels are assumed to be
held for use and exchange. In American pioneer communities
there was always a time when town lots were the chief subject of
commercial activity and men sold and re-sold lots and speculated
in them after the manner of speculation in shares of stock in
commercial centres. But no American court in such an environment ever dreamed of departing from the traditional view
and refusing to enforce specific performance of a contract to
sell a town lot, although there were a hundred like it in every
particular to be had in the real-estate market at a moment's
notice, and its unique character was a transparent dogmatic
fiction. Again, few things in Anglo-American law are more inconvenient than the arbitrary lines between real property and
personal property, running throughout the law, prescribing
distinct rules as to descent and distribution, making a sale of
land subject to one set of doctrines and a sale of chattels subject
to another, and leading to many collateral consequences. English
legislation has made inroads upon the common law in this
respect. But no American court, however much land may have
been a liquid asset in its jurisdiction, ever thought of holding the
common-law attitude toward property in land inapplicable to
local conditions.

Even more significant is the course of American decision
since Professor Bohlen's paper was written. He wrote after
forty years of American discussion of the subject seemed to
have established that the doctrine of *Rylands* v. *Fletcher* would
not be followed in the United States. But the tide began to

turn while he was writing and in the past decade three courts
have accepted it while but one has rejected it. Moreover, when
we look at the jurisdictions which adopt and those which reject
the doctrine, it appears at once that they may not be classified
upon an economic basis. The Supreme Court of Massachusetts
followed the rule in *Rylands* v. *Fletcher* in 1871[1]. It was adopted
by the Supreme Court of Minnesota in the following year[2].
After an interval in which courts had been rejecting it, the rule
was followed in Ohio in 1896, in West Virginia in 1911, in
Missouri in 1911 and in Texas in 1916[3]. It was rejected in New
Hampshire in 1873, in New York in 1873, in New Jersey in
1876, in Pennsylvania in 1886, in California in 1895, in Kentucky
in 1903 and in Indiana in 1911[4]. Agricultural states and industrial states, states with appointed judges holding for life
and elected judges holding for short terms are to be found on
each side. Nor may we explain the decisions in terms of sectional
differences. In New England, Massachusetts and New Hampshire are on opposite sides. In the middle west, the adjoining
states of Ohio and Indiana disagree. In the south, the adjoining
states of West Virginia and Kentucky are on opposite sides.
The Massachusetts court, where the question first came up in
the United States, followed English authority without independent investigation. In New Hampshire, Chief Justice Doe,
one of the great judges of the last century, was not willing to
go upon mere authority and rejected the rule as running counter
to the principle that liability must be based upon fault. The
courts of New York and New Jersey, which have been most
nearly consistent among American courts in applying the
doctrine of no liability without fault, took the same side and

[1] *Shipley* v. *Associates*, 106 *Massachusetts Reports*, 194.
[2] *Cahill* v. *Eastman*, 18 *Minnesota Reports*, 255.
[3] *Defiance Water Co.* v. *Olinger*, 54 *Ohio State Reports*, 532; *Weaver*
v. *Thurmond*, 68 *West Virginia Reports*, 530; *French* v. *Manufacturing Co.*,
173 *Missouri Appeal Reports*, 220, 227; *Texas R. Co.* v. *Frazer* (Texas Court
of Civil Appeals), 182 *Southwestern Reporter*, 1161.
[4] *Brown* v. *Collins*, 53 *New Hampshire Reports*, 442; *Losee* v. *Buchanan*,
51 *New York Reports*, 476; *Marshall* v. *Welwood*, 38 *New Jersey Law Reports*,
339; *Pennsylvania Coal Co.* v. *Sanderson*, 113 *Pennsylvania State Reports*,
126; *Judson* v. *Giant Powder Co.*, 107 *California Reports*, 549; *Owensboro*
v. *Knox*, 116 *Kentucky Reports*, 451; *Lake Shore R. Co.* v. *Chicago R. Co.*,
48 *Indiana Appellate Court Reports*, 584.

for a time their example had a controlling influence. Presently the exigencies of the general security led courts to adopt the rule in several jurisdictions where the question remained open. One may not be so sure that it has been rejected decisively in America as he might have been a generation ago. At any rate the marked revival of the influence of *Rylands* v. *Fletcher* in the United States since 1896 cannot be attributed to an increasing influence of land owners, for the last federal census has established that the balance of population as well as of economic power has passed definitely from rural and agricultural to urban and industrial America.

May it not be that *Rylands* v. *Fletcher*, decided in 1867, is a part of the movement which Dicey has called collectivism, which, he tells us, began to be manifest in 1865?[1] If so, it marks a reaction from the doctrine that liability is to exist only as a corollary of culpability. It subjects the land owner to a liability at his peril, in the interest of the general security. Naturally such a doctrine was announced first in England—in a crowded country where the general security is ever an obvious interest. Naturally also it was received with caution and was rejected for a time in America, where pioneer ideas, appropriate to a less crowded and primarily agricultural country, lingered to the end of the last century. In other words, if the background of the doctrine is in a sense economic, it is not the background of class conflict which has been pictured but is a gradual change in the economic situation, exerting an indirect and gradual and intermittent pressure through a slow alteration in the picture of the end of law which the courts have had before them.

A stock argument for the economic interpretation is derived from the rules of the common law with respect to injuries through the fault of a fellow servant and the doctrine of assumption of risk. These have been pronounced flagrant examples of judicial law-making in the interest of employers and in the teeth of legal principle. But those who make this assertion so confidently take the dogmatic fiction of representation of employer by employee for a premise. They assume that it is

[1] Dicey, *Law and Public Opinion in England*, 250 ff. (1905).

an eternal principle of justice that one who employs another, though not culpable in any wise himself, must be liable for the culpable acts of the other in the course of the employment. What we have is a doctrine of liability without regard to fault imposed upon those who conduct enterprizes by employing others. At bottom the principle is the same as that in the doctrine of *Rylands* v. *Fletcher*—that one who maintains something which if not kept in hand may endanger the general security, must keep it in hand at the risk of responding for resulting injuries if he does not. For juristic purposes this liability was reconciled with the doctrine of no liability without fault by the fiction of representation. The employee was the agent of the employer and his fault was the employer's fault. Taking this fiction at its face value, it was easy to argue that the fellow-servant rule arbitrarily exempted the employer from a just liability. Yet no one who has looked into the subject critically has been deceived thereby[1]. When in the nineteenth century the connection of liability and fault became a settled article of the juristic creed all the historical common-law liabilities without regard to fault were re-examined judicially and for a time there was a strong tendency to limit them. Thus liability for injuries by trespassing animals was limited in *Cox* v. *Burbidge*[2] and more than one American court requires culpability or knowledge of a vicious propensity in such cases[3]. One American court went so far as to require culpability even where there was a known vicious propensity in case the animal escaped in a way not reasonably to be anticipated[4]. The limitation of employer's liability by the fellow-servant rule was a part of this movement. The courts did not arbitrarily set up an exception to a fundamental principle of justice. In the compromise between individual free activity and the general security they had established a liability for fault of employees irrespective of the fault of the employer, a doctrine so far from

---

[1] See Burdick, "Is Law the Expression of Class Selfishness?" 25 *Harvard Law Rev.* 349 (1912).

[2] 13 C.B., N.S. 430 (1863).

[3] *Bischoff* v. *Cheney*, 89 *Connecticut Reports*, 1 (1914); *Peterson* v. *Conlan*, 18 *North Dakota Reports*, 205 (1909).

[4] *De Gray* v. *Murray*, 69 *New Jersey Law Reports*, 458 (1903).

universal that it existed in Roman law only if the employee were a slave and exists in French law in the case of injuries by apprentices only to the extent of a rebuttable presumption that the master was at fault[1]. Having set up this broad liability the courts proceeded to put limits to it. If class self-interest explains the limits, why may we not invoke it to explain the doctrine limited? But this would prove too much.

Not a little of what has been written from the standpoint of the economic interpretation assumes that the grievances, sometimes very real, of industrial labourers against judicial decisions in the nineteenth century are an example of dictation of legal precepts by class interest. But labourers have not been the only persons in society to be aggrieved by the slow response of law to their needs or desires. All who have written upon this subject have assumed that the capitalist class, the captains of industry and the captains of commerce, were the dominant social class at the end of the last century. Hence it is significant that every grievance of the American labourer against American law may be matched by quite as real a grievance of the American business man. The chief instrument by means of which the latter transacts business is the private corporation or business company. If he seeks to do business across a state line by means of that instrument he finds his business potentially an outlaw, suffered to go on solely by the grace of the local authorities. Although the constitution guarantees to him that he may do business over the line, it is interpreted in a way that prevents or hinders him when he seeks to do business in the only way that is practicable for any enterprize of magnitude. If he inquires why this should be so, he finds that it is because at a time when "corporation" meant state-granted monopoly it was decided, rightly enough, that one state could not thrust its monopolies upon another[2]. If he stays at home, he finds himself hampered in the use of this necessary instrument of modern business by a series of traditional legal prejudices and historical limitations which run back to the days when corporation meant munici-

[1] *French Civil Code*, art. 1384; Baudry-Lacantinerie, *Précis de droit civil*, II, 676.
[2] See Henderson, *The Position of Foreign Corporations in American Constitutional Law* (1918).

pality and the king's courts were justly jealous of the powers of such entities and of the way in which those powers were employed[1]. If, instead, he seeks to do business by means of a partnership, an institution as old as commercial activity, and proceeds to keep books showing what he owes the partnership and what the partnership owes him, he is told that legally such things cannot be. The law is not determined by the needs of business nor does it draw its ideas of partnership from the universal understanding and practice of business men. It was fixed centuries ago when Roman jurists sought to understand partnership in terms of the *consortium* of co-heirs after the death of the head of a household[2]. If nineteenth-century courts had been but the mouthpieces through which the business men of America promulgated formulations of their self-interest, these things would have come to an end long ago.

Advocates of the economic interpretation went to the extreme in another respect. As we have seen, all the interpretations that grew out of legal application of Hegel's philosophy of history regarded the course of legal evolution as something inevitable and limited the function of the jurist to historical research and organizing and systematizing, or perhaps predicting, on the basis thereof. But the ethical interpretation and the political interpretation taught that an idea of right and justice or an idea of freedom was guiding the inevitable course of evolution. At least the jurist could use these ideas in his limited task of logical ordering and systematic arrangement. Also the legislator could at least declare and publish the historically developed law in what Bentham called a more "cognoscible" form. The economic interpretation denied them even these limited functions as anything more than hollow pretence. Not only was the course of development inevitable, but judge and jurist and legislator were but spokesmen, conscious or unconscious, of the self-interest of the dominant social class. When they assumed to be more they were deceiving themselves or the public

---

[1] Machen, "Do the Incorporation Laws Allow Sufficient Freedom to Commercial Enterprize?" *Reports of the Maryland State Bar Assoc.* XIV, 78 (1909).
[2] Story, *Commentaries on the Law of Partnership*, § 2 (1841); *Inst.* 2, 25, pr. and §§ 1–2; *Dig.* 17, 2, 63, pr.

or both. It is not likely that law-making will be better than the picture of it we put before the law-maker. Theories of law easily become theories of making law, as is readily verified by observing the effect of the analytical doctrine that law is the command of the sovereign used as a theory of legislation by American legislators[1]. Perhaps one need not say that a more anti-social theory of law-making than that implied in the economic interpretation, as grafted on analytical jurisprudence by American positivists, could not be conceived. A theory of law in terms of the will for the time being of the socially and economically dominant class for the time being, with transitional states of hopeless internal conflict while one class is gaining the upper hand at the expense of its predecessor in the economic and social order, is more threatening to the general security than the eighteenth-century theory of referring all things to the individual conscience as an ultimate arbiter, of which in its nineteenth-century form of philosophical anarchy recent legislation has become so fearful.

Yet it would be a grievous error to reject the economic interpretation wholly because of the extravagances of its advocates. It has an element of truth which we may not ignore and in spite of the recklessness with which it has been urged it has achieved important results. One cannot examine nineteenth-century legislation without perceiving that organized pressure from groups having a common economic interest is the sole explanation of many things upon the statute book. In America legislation allowing a lien to one who furnished material for a building has been pushed to strange lengths through the activities of associations of lumber-dealers[2]. Creditmen's associations have procured laws against the sale of stocks of goods in bulk[3]. Farmers have procured legislation against allowing weeds to go to seed on a railroad right of way wherein the farmer was left free to sow the corners of the earth with seeds from his weed-patches, if he so liked[4]. The remarks of

[1] See Parker, "The Congestion of Law," 29 Report, American Bar Assoc. 383, 387-389 (1906).
[2] See Stimson, American Statute Law, art. 196. Since that compilation many states have pushed such legislation much further.
[3] See note in 33 Harvard Law Rev. 717 (1920).
[4] I have discussed these statutes in "The Revival of Personal Government," Proceedings of the New Hampshire Bar Assoc. 1917, 13.

R.P. 8

Mr Justice Darling about legislation intended to relieve the members of certain organizations from the "humiliatiñg position" of being upon an equality with the rest of the king's subjects might be applied to more than one American statute[1]. Nor may we blind ourselves to the part which the origin, education and every-day associations of the judges have played in the interpretation of laws relating to groups with whose interests they were but imperfectly acquainted, whose aspirations were known to them only in an abstract sense, and whose modes of thought were looked at through the medium of another order of ideas. What seems to me significant is not that now and then we may put our finger upon a decision and explain it in such terms but that such things have had so little influence on the administration of justice and above all so little lasting influence. Nothing could be more eloquent of the efficacy of traditional modes of professional thought and traditional rules of art in holding judges to a reasoned balance of the interests involved and keeping down the influence of suggestion and of subconscious leanings to the minimum which we must expect in all things human.

Among the achievements of the economic interpretation we must put first the effect it has exerted upon ideas as to the end of law. It was no mean service to make us think of satisfaction of wants rather than assertion of wills, to lead jurists to picture a legal ordering of the satisfaction of wants out of the limited material goods of existence in place of a reconciling of wills in action. Again it was a real service to direct attention to the actual operation of codes and traditional bodies of doctrine that ante-dated the industrial organization of the society of today and so took little account of the interests of industrial labourers in such a society[2]. In this respect the economic interpretation was a powerful stimulus to the functional legal science of today.

[1] *Bussey* v. *Amalgamated Society of Railway Servants*, 24 *Times Law Rep.* 437 (1908).
[2] Courey, *Le droit et les ouvriers* (1886); Glasson, *Le code civil et la question ouvrière* (1886); Menger, *Das bürgerliche Recht und die besitzlosen Volksklassen* (1889, 4th ed. 1908); Menger, *Ueber die sozialen Aufgaben des Rechts* (1895, 3rd ed. 1910); Tissier, *Le code civil et les classes ouvrières, Livre du centenaire du code civil Français*, 71–94 (1904); Salvioli, *I difetti sociali del codice civile in relazione alle classe non abbienti ed operaie* (1906).

Again, the idea of a social or sociological legal history, as contrasted with the merely doctrinal or institutional or political legal history of the past, has done much for the science of law. The new edition of Professor Salvioli's history of Italian law shows how much has been gained in this respect in the last decade[1]. Such things as Wigmore's economic-historical interpretation of the English and American law as to confessions show what intelligent use of economic ideas by a master of the legal materials may do for the practical understanding of legal rules[2]. Above all, however, the economic interpretation has been a stimulus to faith in the efficacy of effort, even if its adherents thought juristic effort futile. It has helped to overthrow juristic pessimism by showing the effective power of human action to satisfy human desires, even if it exaggerated the extent to which men had deliberately shaped the law to attain class ends.

[1] "The purpose of this work is to follow the development of Italian law in its various manifestations of time and place, ever keeping it in touch with the social ground in which it was formed, with the atmosphere in which it lives, and so with Italian society in its economic, political, religious and moral life. Hence in writing the history of Italian law I have had in view also the writing of the social, economic, and juridical history of the Italian people, at least in its chief lines, in an organic and indivisible whole." Salvioli, *Storia del diritto Italiano*, 8th ed., preface (1921).

[2] *Evidence*, I, § 865 (1904).

VI

THE GREAT-LAWYER INTERPRETATION

EACH of the interpretations heretofore considered lays hold of a single factor of more or less importance in the process of adjusting the legal materials handed down from the civilization of the past to the demands of the civilization of the present and of finding or creating new materials and fitting them with the old into a more or less harmonious system, where the traditional materials are refractory or insufficient or their possibilities are unknown or misunderstood. Behind the ethical interpretation is the truth that men have sought to make the administration of justice and the laws by which it is administered conform to ideas of right and that their endeavours to do so have in large measure succeeded. The legal order has been able to maintain itself, law has been able to supersede the older agencies of social control and has become the chief agency thereof, to which others are subordinated, because these efforts have been so persistent and in consequence so successful.

Behind the political interpretation is the truth that more and more since the sixteenth century and universally in the nineteenth century the end of law was conceived in terms of the maximum of individual self-assertion. This end was to be attained through a politico-legal ordering of society in which coercive social control was reduced to its lowest terms. Self-assertion is one of the fundamental instincts or, if you will, one of the fundamental desires of men. There is ample experience of how serious the consequences may be if men's aspirations for free self-assertion are repressed beyond a reasonable compromise required for the securing of other social interests. The conception of law as a necessary evil, the doctrine that each rule of law must be justified by showing that it promotes a maximum of individual self-assertion, the doctrine of a minimum of law, restricted to what is demonstrably necessary to the realization of freedom as an idea, are protests against legal repression for the sake of a rational scheme rationally carried out, to which eighteenth-century thinking had seemed to lead. The recognition of the social interest in the individual life which is so marked in recent legislation, in recent judicial decision and above all in recent juristic thought, is a new and more inclusive way of putting for the purposes of today what the historical school sought to put for the last century in its idea of "freedom."

There was something also behind the positivist interpretations which gave them plausibility and enabled them to maintain themselves. Physical environment may not be ignored by jurist or legal historian. Such things as the Roman law of public and private streams and the modern refilling of the content of those terms in another way[1], as the English and the American criteria of admiralty jurisdiction[2], as the definition of a navigable stream in England and America respectively[3], as the English, the so-called California and the so-called Colorado theories as to the use of water of a running stream[4], or as the English and the Australasian[5] views as to flood waters, speak for themselves. It would be rash to say that race psychology must not enter profoundly into all consideration of what legal precepts may be imposed effectively upon this or that people. Behind the biological interpretations in terms of conflict of instincts is the truth that the problem of the legal order is at bottom one of reconciling or harmonizing or compromising conflicting or overlapping interests—that is, conflicting or overlapping human claims or demands or desires—and that the pressure of this conflict compels continual change in the details of the legal order. Behind the economic interpretation is the truth that these claims or demands or desires have to do chiefly with applying the material goods of existence to the satisfaction of human wants.

One element, however, is rejected or ignored. None of the

---

[1] *Dig.* 43, 12, 1, § 3; *French Civil Code*, art. 538.

[2] "The Genesee Chief," 12 *Howard's Reports* (U.S.), 443 (1851).

[3] *Carson* v. *Blazer*, 2 *Binney's Reports* (Pennsylvania), 475 (1807); *Browne* v. *Chadbourne*, 31 *Maine Reports*, 9 (1849).

[4] *Embrey* v. *Owen*, 6 Exch. 353 (1851); *Elliot* v. *Fitchburg R. Co.*, 10 *Cushing's Reports* (Massachusetts), 191 (1852); *Lux* v. *Haggin*, 69 *California Reports*, 255 (1895); *Hammond* v. *Rose*, 11 *Colorado Reports*, 524 (1887).

[5] *Gerrard* v. *Crowe* [1921], 1 A.C. 395.

nineteenth-century interpretations will hear of an element of creative activity of men as lawyers, judges, writers of books, or legislators. They have nothing to say about juristic endeavours to reconcile or harmonize or compromise overlapping claims by creative reason or an inventive process of trial and error. They think of the phenomena of legal development as events, as if men were not acting in the bringing about of every one of them. For the so-called events of legal history are in truth acts of definite men or even of a definite man. The praetor's edict was not a self-evolving thing. Some one applied to a praetor for a remedy and persuaded him to grant it with the result that a clause was added to the edict with the significant words *actionem dabo*. In such a situation there are three things to consider, the men who acted, the materials on or with which they acted and the conditions in which they acted. The nineteenth-century interpretations left the men out entirely, at least in their quality of men. The historical jurists did not think of the man who acted. At most they thought of a whole race and of the man as but a particular sample as it were of a stock pattern of men with a stock spirit. All of these interpretations in one way or another explain law in terms of the conditions of action not in terms of the actor; in terms of something external to the actor whereby his action was mere appearance masking the operations of the reality in the background. They think of man in the abstract, not of men. The real actors are formulae. As Cuoco said of a like type of interpretation of general history, letters of the alphabet might as well be substituted for the names of the so-called actors[1].

For example, consider Dicey's interpretation of English law in the nineteenth century[2], perhaps the soberest and broadest that has been written. It is an economic-political interpretation in terms of public opinion. Public opinion, with economic changes behind it, changed slowly and through political institutions and movements brought about changes in the law. We have seen in the last decade that public opinion does not

[1] *Saggio storico*, preface to 2nd ed.
[2] *Lectures on the Relation between Law and Public Opinion in England in the Nineteenth Century* (1905, 2nd ed. 1914).

evolve itself nor is it generated spontaneously by economic changes. Men, preaching and arguing and writing and teaching and haranguing, are active agents in producing it and in recent years we have had many illustrations of the extent to which it may be manufactured deliberately and on a large scale. Indeed the wholesale manufacture of public opinion as a means to this or that end has become a business, and organizations exist with wide-spread ramifications whose real purpose is to bring about a factitious public opinion. For that matter official gazettes and bulletins and spectacles had not been unknown heretofore and inquisitions and censorships and restrictions upon teaching, and prosecutions for seditious agitation, and other forms of preventing the manufacture of public opinion of a sort inconvenient to the ruling group of men for the time being, have always existed. Behind public opinion are human desires and wants and claims making themselves felt through human beings upon human beings and leading the latter to act in the administration of justice, in juristic writing and in legislation. Surely the men who are active in this process may not be ignored if we are to understand it fully.

Omission of men from our juristic reckonings in the nineteenth century bore fruit in the jurisprudence of conceptions, as Jhering called it[1], which was so conspicuous not only in the juristic writing but in the actual administration of justice during the hegemony of the historical school. A historically derived conception was the whole measure of judicial action. The conception was not to be fitted to the case so as to bring about a result in that particular case by which the law might be given effect with reference to its end. The result in the particular case was immaterial. The case was to be fitted to the conception after the manner of Procrustes. It was the boast of the Romanist that the legal conceptions to be found in the writings of the Roman jurists of the third century sufficed for the solution of every legal problem of today. It was the belief of the Anglo-American historical jurist that like universally valid conceptions

[1] *Scherz und Ernst in der Jurisprudenz*, pt. 3 (1884), 10th ed., 245 ff. See Pound, "Mechanical Jurisprudence," 8 *Columbia Law Rev.* 605 (1909); Holmes, *Collected Papers*, 231–232.

were derivable from the Year Books, by which questions arising in the law of today might be answered[1]. Jhering said that the legal conceptions of the historical school required a world of their own in which they existed wholly for themselves, far from every connection with life[2]. They were not actual Roman[3] nor actual medieval English legal institutions. They were abstract creations with no relation to the life of the past nor to that of the present.

Some examples will bring this out. Thus, the doctrine of *Victorian Railways* v. *Coultas*[4], now happily overruled in England but still raising its head in the United States, denied recovery for fright or mere mental injury, however manifest in physical consequences, unless the causal nexus was vouched for by intention to injure or by some physical impact at the time the fright or mental suffering was culpably produced. In reality this was a practical rule, growing out of the limitations of trial by jury, the difficulty of proof in cases of injuries manifest subjectively only and the backwardness of our knowledge with respect to the relations of mind and body. In view of the danger of imposition, the courts, on a balance of the interests involved, refused to go beyond cases where there was a voucher for the truth of the plaintiff's claim, either in the intention of the defendant to bring about such a result or in a physical impact which in ordinary experience was known to have such results[5]. With the rise of modern psychology the basis of this caution in securing an important element of the interest of personality

---

[1] E.g. Ames, *Lectures on Legal History*, 172, 191, and the theoretical development, 192 ff. (written 1889–1890). See Professor Bordwell's comments in 34 *Harvard Law Rev.* 740 (1921).

[2] "The sphere in which the theoretical beyond is placed does not belong to the solar system. No ray of light shines therein. The sun is the source of all life; but conceptions do not concern themselves with life. They require a world of their own in which they exist wholly for themselves, far from every connection with life." Jhering, *Scherz und Ernst in der Jurisprudenz*, 10th ed., 247.

[3] See Savigny, *System des heutigen römischen Rechts*, 1, § 35 (1840).

[4] 13 App. Cas. 222 (1888).

[5] "The point is not put as a logical deduction from the general principles of liability in tort, but as a limitation of those principles on purely practical grounds." Holmes, C.J., in *Smith* v. *Postal T. Co.*, 174 *Massachusetts Reports*, 576 (1899). See also the observations of the same judge in *Homans* v. *Boston E. R. Co.*, 180 *Massachusetts Reports*, 456 (1902).

was removed. But in the meantime a legal conception had come into being. The doctrine had been rested upon a conception of a right of physical integrity as including integrity of the physical person but not mere peace of mind[1]. This conception had been verified historically and the rule now stood intrenched. To show the falsity of the assumption that nothing physical was involved in fright made no difference. We were not dealing with the facts of human life but with conceptions that were self-sufficient.

Again, take the much-discussed case of an injury to the mother of an unborn child whereby the child is born maimed[2]. This was solved by the conception that legal personality begins with birth. Hence there was no legal personality in the child when the injury to the mother took place and after the child's legal personality had come into being no injury was done it. We may understand caution in allowing recovery in such cases because of the difficulty of establishing a causal relation between the injury and the condition of the child at birth. But this way of looking at cases was alien to nineteenth-century modes of thought. All must rest on the legal conception. There was no suggestion of turning to medical science to ascertain the actual situation for which the legal rule must be made. Law was eternally self-sufficient. It was not to change as medical or psychological knowledge increased, since from its conception the legal rule must be fixed once for all—from the beginning and to eternity.

Again, suppose that in such a case as *Dulieu* v. *White*[3], two women were in the room, one of whom owned the house while the other was her guest. According to some decisions, proceeding in the purely mechanical fashion of the jurisprudence of conceptions, the one could have recovered damages for the miscarriage produced by the negligently caused fright, since she might have claimed them as an item of damages for the

[1] See Bohlen, "Right to Recover for Injury Resulting from Injury without Impact," 41 *American Law Register*, 141, 142–144 (1902).
[2] *Walker* v. *Great Northern R. Co.*, L.R. 28 Ir. 69; *Dietrich* v. *Northampton*, 138 *Massachusetts Reports*, 14; *Allaire* v. *St Luke's Hospital*, 184 *Illinois Reports*, 359; *Gorman* v. *Budlong*, 23 *Rhode Island Reports*, 169.
[3] [1901] 2 K.B. 669.

trespass upon her land, while the other could not recover. Or again, if a horse not known to be vicious trespassed on land and kicked the owner of the land, he could recover. But there is authority for saying that if it also kicked a third person casually but rightfully on the land, the latter could not recover[1]. Or, if in blasting operations, carried on with due care, stones were unexpectedly cast on another's land and hit both the owner of the land and another person casually but rightfully there, we were told that the one might recover as an additional item of damage for the trespass, but the other might not recover at all. For if one were allowed to cast stones on another's land, even though without negligence, without liability, he might acquire a servitude of so doing, whereas there could be no acquisition of a servitude of casting stones on a human being. Such a condition of the law so offended the common sense of the New York Court of Appeals that it took the bull by the horns and allowed the person casually on the land to recover also, despite its cherished principle of no liability without fault; saying that life and limb were at least as sacred as property and that if the owner of the land might recover, the injured non-owner must recover also[2]. The legal basis of such a recovery is still in much doubt. But the judges did not wait for the idea. In this case they acted on instinct.

An English example may be seen in the cases of *Winterbottom* v. *Wright*[3] and *George* v. *Skivington*[4]. According to these cases and as a result of the conception of liability as arising only between the parties to a sale, if a manufacturer negligently sells you a defective automobile negligently manufactured, not knowing of the defect and the defect being latent, if you are injured you may recover. If you give it to your brother and he goes out in it and is injured, he may not recover. But if, when you buy it you tell the manufacturer that you are buying it for your brother and then he goes out in it and is injured, he may recover.

[1] *Troth* v. *Wills*, 8 *Pennsylvania Superior Court Reports*, 1 (1898); *Bischoff* v. *Cheney*, 89 *Connecticut Reports*, 1 (1914).

[2] *Sullivan* v. *Dunham*, 161 *New York Reports*, 290, 294. See Smith, "Liability for Damage by Blasting," 33 *Harvard Law Rev.* 542, 667 (1920).

[3] 10 M. & W. 109 (1842).

[4] L. R. 5 Exch. 1 (1869). Sir Frederick Pollock speaks of this as "not a very profitable case." *Torts*, 11th ed., note *h*.

This sort of thing is not as well regarded in the law as it was in the middle of the last century; as it was, for example, in the days of imputed negligence[1]. It is a welcome sign of the times that when legal conceptions were pressed upon the New York Court of Appeals recently and it was asked to hold that where a spring board projected from a railroad right of way over a river where the public had a right to bathe, as the spring board was annexed to the right of way and hence was a fixture, a man on the end over the river was technically a trespasser and so was not protected from the negligence of the railroad company —when asked to apply logic to legal conceptions in this way, the court denounced the jurisprudence of conceptions and refused to carry out the conception of a fixture and the conception of trespass to such a result[2].

American constitutional law is full of the jurisprudence of conceptions. A conception of liberty of contract as due process of law and a conception of the police power—a conception of a maximum of individual self-assertion and of a legislative power to restrict such self-assertion for the public health or safety or morals—for a time replaced the standard of reasonableness with reference to the circumstances of time and place for which the rule was enacted and to which it was to be applied[3]. Thus in one of the truck-act cases already referred to a statute required corporations employing ten or more persons to pay wages in cash. The court said this was unconstitutional as putting the labourer under guardianship and imposing an incapacity by an "arbitrary fiat[4]." Equity had seen the *de facto* inequality between fiduciary and beneficiary and between lender and borrower because of the advantageous position of the former in each case. The common-law courts had seen the *de facto* inequality between public utility and patron. Courts and legislatures had seen the *de facto* inequality between insurance company and insured. In such cases and many more like them the law had regulated the contracts which the parties might

[1] *Thorogood* v. *Bryan*, 8 C.B. 115 (1849).
[2] *Hynes* v. *New York Central R. Co.*, 231 *New York Reports*, 229, 235 (1921).
[3] See Pound, "Liberty of Contract," 18 *Yale Law Journ.*, 454 (1909).
[4] Smith, J., in *State* v. *Haun*, 61 *Kansas Reports*, 146, 161 ff. (1900).

make in these relations in order to insure that no advantage should be taken of the actual inequality and that the contracts made should be fair. But the legislature could not recognize the *de facto* advantage of employer over employee where the employer was a mining corporation because that advantage had not yet taken form in a legal conception. It was but *de facto*. To recognize it was "arbitrary." Legal conceptions were like Lewis Carroll's watch. Facts had no more effect upon the one than time upon the other[1].

Ideas may require such things. But men revolt against them and this revolt of men is one cause of legal development. The facts affect men even if ideas are impervious; and men reshape or reject the conceptions accordingly. This reaction of men to facts, directed more or less by a traditional technique and along more or less logical lines, not the internal self-developing force of the conceptions, has fashioned legal institutions and rules and doctrines.

May we interpret law and legal history in terms of the element which the last century ignored? Is it possible to make a great-lawyer interpretation of legal history? May we tell the story around the personality of judges and law-givers and jurists? If we may do so, how far is the interpretation valid? Lord Campbell suggested such an interpretation. But his project of writing the history of English law and of the English constitution around the lives of the Chancellors and the Chief

[1] For other cases of the "jurisprudence of conceptions," see the decisions discussed by Dean Wigmore in "Contributory Negligence as a Bar to an Administrator's Action for Death," 2 *Illinois Law Rev.* 487–494. Dean Wigmore's comments are in point. He says: "To say that the nominal parties only will be considered, no matter what justice may require, is to say that law consists in the mechanical operation of certain steel cogs and levers, or in the mathematical solution of a certain equation of a, m, n, and x, no matter what the result is in justice" (p. 487). "But to get at justice, perhaps by changing the tools or by mending the machine, or by inventing an eccentric to replace a simple circular rotation—somehow to get results, in short—this, the genius of adaptiveness, which has marked so marvellously the industrial achievements of our nation and has given us a distinguished character among the world's peoples—this genius seems to fail us when we enter the halls of justice. The failure to exercise it is a feature of all the courts. ...The courts that favor recovery and the courts that oppose recovery are alike affected by it. Whichever attitude they take, their method is a mechanical one; they cannot apportion, they cannot adjust; they will merely work out a formula." (p. 494).

Justices[1] was executed merely as a series of superficial but entertaining biographies, and his anachronistic method of writing history—as, for example, in writing an eighteenth-century charge to a jury for a chief justice in a trial for treason under Edward IV[2]—has created prejudice against the whole method. Moreover legal history began to be written on a large scale in the nineteenth century and so under the influence of Savigny and also and chiefly of Hegel. Hence, it came to be written sometimes avowedly and sometimes unconsciously in terms of ideas not of men. Yet Lord Campbell's instinct, as a lawyer and judge who had been at work for more than a generation in the laboratories where law was making and had seen and experienced the part that men and their characters and personalities played in the work done in those laboratories and in fashioning their output—Lord Campbell's instinct was sound. We cannot think of lawyers and judges and legislators merely as the passive instruments of ideas. We must recognize that great minds and masterful personalities will at least help to explain many things in legal history.

Something not unlike the great-lawyer interpretation may be seen in current thinking about law in two stages of legal development, namely, in primitive law, the fluid stage before the strict law, and in the stage of equity and natural law, the fluid stage that succeeds to the strict law. In primitive law the body of legal precepts is frequently attributed to a god or to a divinely inspired prophet or sage or the whole body of legal and political institutions is attributed to some one law-giver. Thus the Hebrew law was attributed to Moses[3], the laws and institutions of Sparta were ascribed to Lycurgus, Roman legal and political institutions of a military character were referred to Romulus and those of a religious character to Numa. No doubt in part this is an attempt to put symbolically the sacredness of law or the antiquity and authority of the custom on

---

[1] "The history of the holders of the Great Seal is the history of our constitution as well as of our jurisprudence." Lord Campbell, *Lives of the Lord Chancellors*, preface to first edition, p. v (1845).

[2] *Lives of the Chief Justices*, I, 149–150.

[3] A convenient discussion of this may be found in Kent, *Israel's Laws and Legal Precedents* (1907).

which the general security rests. No doubt also it is connected with an instinctive human tendency to see a personality like ourselves behind all phenomena; to find a malignant spirit behind those events of nature that thwart or injure us and a beneficent spirit behind those which further or satisfy our desires. This tendency remains strong among men despite education and science. In the conduct of legal and political institutions the common mode of thought is to find some one good man behind the doing of things well and some one bad man behind the doing of things ill. Our political institutions involving personal competition between political leaders further this. But it is innate and persistent. With all allowances for such causes, however, it is significant that attributing of law to definite conscious human law-givers belongs to the two stages of vigorous creative activity. For in the classical period of the Roman law we find the same idea, partly, perhaps, as something handed down from an earlier stage of legal development, but asserted by men who were subjecting everything to the test of reason[1]. Also we find it well marked in the analogous stage of modern law, the hegemony of the law-of-nature school in the seventeenth and eighteenth centuries. The wise law-giver who discovered the dictates of reason, formulated them for his people, and enacted them as a code, was the favourite theme of the legal historian of that time[2]. On the other hand in the strict law and in what I have called the maturity of law, legal history is interpreted not in terms of creation but in terms of authority; in the strict law in terms of authority as such, in the maturity of law in the nineteenth century in terms of historical or metaphysical or observed and verified authority in the form of an idea or a law of development.

In other words, interpretation in terms of creative activity

[1] E.g. in the sketch of Roman legal history by Pomponius in the *Digest*, the fixed forms of *legis actiones* are ascribed to the Decemvirs (*Dig.* 1, 1, 2, § 6); Sextus Aelius is said to have "composed additional forms" (*id.* § 7); it is said that Labeo "undertook to make a good many innovations" (*id.* § 47).

[2] "Just as we are apt to impute the invention of this [the jury] and some other pieces of judicial polity to the superior genius of Alfred the Great; to whom, on account of his having done much, it is usual to attribute everything." Blackstone, *Commentaries*, III, 349 (1765).

belongs to periods of growth by development of new institutions and by absorption or infusion from without. Interpretation in terms of authority or philosophical substitutes for authority belongs to periods of rigidity and stability. The writing of legal history remained Hegelian long after history-writing at large had been delivered from the philosophy of history. Perhaps a Freudian might explain this consistent ignoring of the creative element, of the element of human action, in the legal science of the nineteenth century. For nineteenth-century jurists sought to eliminate the personal element in the administration of justice. They sought to eliminate all individualization of application. They put their faith in a closed system of rules mechanically developed by inflexible logic and mechanically administered. It would have been highly inconvenient to recognize a personal creative element in the origin or operation of this closed system and in the fashioning and setting up of its institutions. Hence that element was not seen and the assumption of a self-developing legal history was put behind the assumption of a mechanically self-acting law.

Let us think for a moment in the way which the last century rejected. Let us think of men striving to do justice, to satisfy demands, to secure social interests. We are not bound to believe that they make legal precepts and set up legal institutions out of whole cloth. Except as an act of Omnipotence, creation does not mean the making of something out of nothing. Creative activity takes materials and gives them form so that they may be put to uses for which the materials unformed are not adapted. Let us think, then, of men striving to do justice and satisfy demands and secure social interests by principles of reason, in order to eliminate the wilfulness and personal caprice which was a chief menace to the general security in ancient society. Let us think of them as striving to do these things with the legal materials that had come down to them, held back by a belief in authority in some one of its main forms—divine, customary, rational or logical—held back by consciousness that their action in the course of this striving would be judged by the opinion of their fellow men or later criticized by a profession trained in a traditional mode of thought and traditional rules of art, and held back by traditional modes of thought and rules of art that kept them for the most part within certain limits and to a more or less fixed technique of treating more or less fixed materials. Let us think of them as breaking these bonds from time to time in bursts of creative activity when existing materials would not suffice for pressing demands and the fixed technique proved inadequate to supply new ones. Let us think of them also as held fast by these bonds in alternating periods of legal stability, in which, however, growth and creation and invention go on slowly on a smaller scale and within narrower lines.

In the process so sketched, now and then a masterful personality chooses between possible materials in the existing stock or between possible ways of using them, imposes his choice upon his generation and thus stamps the materials with which succeeding generations will work. Or a masterful personality overhauls the traditional modes of thought and rules of art, the technique with which succeeding generations will work upon the given legal materials, recasts them to his ideas or prejudices or temperament, and thus imposes his personal attitude and his personal character upon the law for a long time to come. It was in this way that Coke had so enduring an influence upon our law. As it were, the spectacles through which we see the traditional materials of the old English law were made to fit Coke's particular astigmatism. Had the spectacles been Bacon's not Coke's, had Bacon's quest for early professional advancement been successful—as might well have been in view of his abilities and connections—had he risen to high judicial office before and not behind Coke and given direction to our legal development at a critical point, or had his project for codification been taken up by the king, one has only to read that project[1] to perceive that the history of our law in the next three centuries would have looked very different.

A legal history that sees law only as it is expounded in juristic treatises will give no consideration to such questions. For the juristic treatise may be compared to a herbarium. In the herbarium typical forms—that is forms chosen by the collector

---

[1] "Proposition to His Majesty Touching the Compilation and Amendment of the Laws of England," Spedding, *Letters and Life of Bacon*, VI, 61–71.

because they conform most nearly to a picture he has made himself—are pressed and dried and classified and an ideal vegetation is written upon that basis. It helps us to understand plants undoubtedly. But it falls to pieces as a description of nature whenever one looks attentively at the facts of nature in the field. Herbarium species are related to the variety of individual form in nature as the ideal legal conceptions and the ideal legal institutions of the lawyer's books are related to the unceasing variety of phenomena that goes on in the actual administration of justice. Whether or not men count in the law as set forth in the books, they count powerfully in the law in action. For the purpose of fixing types and ordering and classifying and endeavouring to put the phenomena of justice or some part of them in the order of reason, the jurist must ignore men. He must think of the legal conception or the legal precept or the legal principle as the systematic botanist thinks of the species—in terms of an idea, not as a core of consistency in a mass of phenomena shading out to a no-man's-land in every direction. The practising lawyer on the other hand knows painfully how much depends upon the particular judge on whose list his case chances to be; he understands well how much depends upon who argues a case before a given tribunal; he appreciates how much the result hangs upon the personnel of the appellate tribunal before which a decisive battle of the law chanced to be waged. For the purposes of juristic analysis it is no matter who argued a case before Vice-Chancellor Shadwell with which the student of equity must reckon as an authority to be reconciled or developed in a system of that subject. Yet a student of the memoirs of contemporary lawyers may derive light upon a hard point when he notes that the cause was argued by Sugden or Knight Bruce or Bethell[1].

With all its talk of evolution, nineteenth-century jurisprudence and particularly nineteenth-century mechanical-positivist jurisprudence was comparable to the biology of special creation.

---

[1] "The tyranny which successive leaders exercised over Shadwell would be inconceivable to those who did not witness it. The earliest of them was Sugden....From him the sceptre passed to Knight Bruce....He was succeeded as Lord of Sir Lancelot Shadwell's Court by Bethell." Lord Selborne, *Memorials Family and Personal*, I, 374–376 (1896).

In each case the fundamental assumption is that all the main lines had been laid out once for all. There could be nothing more than relatively trifling variations within the narrow lines of species created from the beginning. The herbarium belongs to the Linnaean or pre-Darwinian botany of specially created species. In the same way the nineteenth-century analytical jurisprudence, as anything more than an instrument to be used as one of many instruments, belongs to a pre-evolutionary type of legal thought. The text-book of analytical jurisprudence is a legal herbarium.

Creative law-making, inventive activity to devise new institutions, provide new precepts and find new principles, takes the form of setting up procedural fictions, or later of use of the wider and more general fictions of interpretation, equity and natural law; the form of judicial empiricism, or process of trial and error or inclusion and exclusion by judicial decision; the form of juristic science and the form of legislation. In the case of many procedural fictions, which were effective to produce important changes of substance, we know who devised them and how the exigencies of meeting a special case where existing legal materials were inadequate moved him to do so. Thus the *actio Publiciana*, one of the revolutionary procedural fictions of the Roman law, bears the name of its author. Again the history of the curious fiction of American federal procedure, whereby corporations are permitted to sue in federal courts as citizens of the state in which they are incorporated, is well known[1]. It shows a somewhat crude inventive activity on the

---

[1] At first it was said that a corporation aggregate could not sue in the federal courts unless because of the citizenship of the natural persons who composed it. *Hope Ins. Co.* v. *Boardman*, 5 *Cranch's Reports* (U.S.), 57 (1809); *Bank of the United States* v. *Deveaux, id.* 61; *Commercial Bank* v. *Slocomb*, 14 *Peters' Reports* (U.S.), 60 (1840). Next it was held that the suit "was presumed to be a suit by or against citizens of the state which created the corporate body" and that no averment or evidence to the contrary was receivable. *Ohio R. Co.* v. *Wheeler*, 1 *Black's Reports* (U.S.), 286 (1861); *Louisville R. Co.* v. *Letson*, 2 *Howard's Reports* (U.S.), 497 (1844). At length the courts held that a corporation "is a citizen of the state which created it." *St Louis* v. *Wiggins Ferry Co.*, 11 *Wallace's Reports*, 423 (1870); *Chicago R. Co.* v. *Whitton*, 13 *Wallace's Reports*, 270 (1871). See Henderson, *The Position of Foreign Corporations in American Constitutional Law*, 39–60. It should be remembered in this connection that in American legal parlance "corporation" includes limited companies formed by agreement under general laws.

part of judges confronted with a situation in which as the law stood they could not give effect to claims or demands which appealed to them as deserving to be secured. Here are creative devices of far-reaching effect which did not evolve spontaneously but were deliberately made by known men to meet definite demands in concrete cases. The idea of equitable ownership did not create the *actio Publiciana*. It was a later juristic deduction[1].

Procedural fictions are succeeded as creative agencies in law-making by the bolder and more general fictions of interpretation, equity and natural law. Austin showed long ago that only a small part of what goes by the name of interpretation is a genuine search for the intent of the rule as it was framed[2]. It is because cases arise which were not within the purview of that intent that interpretation so-called becomes one of the most difficult of judicial tasks[3]. When justice must be administered within the four corners of a rigid code or by means of a body of customary law which has attained fixity in the stage of the strict law, the only resource in the absence of legislative revolution, from which men shrink, is to find by interpretation the needed rules which the body of existing legal precepts does not provide but which the court requires if it is to administer justice. The fiction that a sacred or authoritative text means what it palpably did not mean or covers what no one had in mind when it was promulgated, is but a further step in the direction already taken by procedural fictions. For in this type of interpretation the thing found was first put into the text and then drawn forth with an air of discovery. In every stage of legal development this sort of interpretation has been one of the main resources of courts and jurists. Restrained by a traditional technique expressed in maxims and canons, both in the Roman law and in

[1] The term "bonitary ownership" appears first in the sixth century. Theophilus on *Inst.* 1, 5, 3.

[2] *Jurisprudence*, 3rd ed., 1023–1036. See Pound, "Spurious Interpretation," 7 *Columbia Law Rev.* 379 (1907). Compare: "The power of *interpretatio* and formulation placed in the hands of the Pontiffs was in effect a power to alter the law by ingenious interpretations....There is not much to be said for the logic of these interpretations, but there can be no doubt of their utility." Buckland, *Roman Law*, 2.

[3] Gray, *Nature and Sources of the Law*, §§ 370–399 (1909).

our own law, it has proved equal to the most refractory materials of the legal system, and in other bodies of law the most rigid codes and the most stringent provisions against judicial glossing or developing of their texts have yielded to it. One need only refer to such things as the interpretation of the *Lex Aquilia*, which in the end made over the whole theory of delictual liability, or Coke's juristic law-making by interpretation of Magna Carta and of the statutes of Edward I, in proof of its creative possibilities. But here again the process is not one that goes on automatically. It is not a logical unfolding of what is implicit in the text. In the case of Coke's Second Institute and the interpretation of English legislation of the thirteenth century, we know who it was that made a body of law for modern England and for America on the basis of these crude and sometimes oracular texts and why he did so. Coke's purpose was to prove his case in the contests between courts and crown in which he was a chief actor. Recent historians who have re-examined the material in writing histories of the King's Council, the Star Chamber and the High Commission, assert that he grossly perverted the texts[1]. Very likely he did for he was a partisan and an advocate. Undoubtedly he did from their standpoint because they are asking what the provisions meant to those who drew them in the thirteenth century for thirteenth-century England. Coke's problem was what they must be made to mean if justice was to be done in accordance with them and by means of them in seventeenth-century England. The fiction of interpretation enabled him and his contemporaries to believe that the two things were the same.

Equity and natural law are yet bolder fictions allowing a more sweeping creative activity. Maine showed this for equity generally and Langdell and Maitland showed it for English equity[2]. The chancellor did not purport to alter the law. According to the law the penalty of a bond was enforceable, the estate of the mortgagee after condition unfulfilled was absolute,

---

[1] Usher, *The Rise and Fall of the High Commission*, 186–187, 191–192, 199–201, 222–235 (1913).

[2] Maine, *Ancient Law*, chap. 3 (1861); Langdell, *Brief Survey of Equity Jurisdiction*, 13 ff. (written 1887); Maitland, *Equity and the Forms of Action at Common Law*, 19 ff. (1909).

the legal ownership of the trustee was complete and unchallenge-able. But above the legal measure there was a higher criterion of equity and good conscience, governing the exercise of his legal rights and powers by the creditor or mortgagee or trustee, and imposing duties upon his conscience which the chancellor undertook to enforce by preventing him from exacting more than his damages or compelling him to allow redemption or compelling him to hold and use and administer the property for the benefit of *cestui que trust*. In many of the cases in which equity has interfered in this way, saving the face of the law but wholly changing the practical working of the legal system, we know the very chancellor who first acted and the very state of facts that moved him to act[1]. As Maitland has said, the chancellor was not troubled about ideas and general theories. The defendant's conduct was gross dishonesty and he had simply to find an effective remedial device that might be enforced *in personam*[2]. The Institutes tell a like story as to enforcement of testamentary trusts in Roman law. Augustus was moved to interfere out of favour to particular persons and in certain cases of gross fraud[3].

Natural law, the great agency of juristic development of law, is a fiction of a superior body of legal principles, existing in reason, of which the actual body of law is but an imperfect reflection and by which, therefore, the actual law may be corrected and supplemented. The theory is an expression of the jurisconsult's desire to improve and to add to the existing legal materials, in order to achieve definite ends in litigation, without impairing confidence in the law as of unchallengeable

[1] " I intentionally say modern rules because it must not be forgotten that the rules of Courts of Equity are not, like the rules of the common law, sup-posed to have been established from time immemorial. It is perfectly well known that they have been established from time to time—altered, refined and improved from time to time. In many cases we know the names of the Chancellors who invented them. No doubt they were invented for the purpose of securing the better administration of justice, but still they wer invented. Take such things as these: the separate use of a married woman, the restraint on alienation, the modern rule against perpetuities and the rules of equitable waste. We can name the Chancellors who first invented them, and state the date when they were first introduced into equity jurisprudence." Jessel, M.R., in *Hallett's Estate*, 13 Ch.D. 696, 710 (1879).

[2] Maitland, *Equity*, 30.

[3] *Inst*. 2, 23, 1.

authority and in such a way as to persuade tribunals to accept his results. I need not remind you of what Roman jurists were able to do with this instrument. Continental jurists did like things with the same instrument in the seventeenth and eighteenth centuries[1].

Judicial empiricism has done for the common law most of what was done for the Roman law by juristic science. Usually it proceeds cautiously from case to case with an occasional creative generalization. But there are many cases of creative judicial action which has made new chapters in the law or new legal institutions almost at a stroke. One such case may be seen in the decisions of Lord Mansfield combining ideas of English equity and Roman texts as to unjust enrichment, applying them to the common counts, and giving us a fruitful principle of what we call, not happily, quasi contract[2]. Another case is the addition of a new chapter to the law of servitudes by Lord Cottenham's decision in *Tulk* v. *Moxhay*[3]. Here again the decision grew out of the exigencies of justice in a concrete case. So far was it from being the product of the unfolding of an abstract idea, that the reasoning of Lord Cottenham, proceeding on a theory of preventing unjust enrichment, is obviously fallacious and has been abandoned for a theory of equitable servitudes[4]. But the new chapter in the law of property stands. American law may furnish an example in the institution known as the Juvenile Court. This institution, which is making its way everywhere, is due to the initiative of a few definitely

[1] "The principles of the Roman law respecting the different kinds of agreements and the distinction between contracts and simple agreements, not being founded on the law of nature and being, indeed, very remote from simplicity, are not admitted into our law." Pothier, *Traité des Obligations*, pt. I, chap. I, art. I (1761).

[2] "This kind of equitable action to recover back money which ought not in justice to be kept, is very beneficial and therefore much encouraged....In one word the gist of this kind of action is that the defendant, upon the circumstances of the case, is obliged by the ties of natural justice and equity to refund the money." *Moses* v. *Macferlan*, 2 Burr. 1005, 1012 (1760). As to Lord Mansfield's creative work in commercial law, see Buller, J., in *Lickbarrow* v. *Mason*, 2 T.R. 63; Story, *Miscellaneous Works*, 411–412; Lord Campbell, *Lives of the Chief Justices*, II, chap. 34.

[3] 2 Phil. 774 (1848).

[4] *Rogers* v. *Hosegood* [1900] 2 Ch. 388; *In re Nisbet and Potts' Contract* [1905] 1 Ch. 391, 399, [1906] 1 Ch. 386, 401, 405, 409.

known socially-minded judges, who had the large vision to see what was required and the good sense not to be hindered in doing it because there had never been such things before. Today we find a legal basis for it in the jurisdiction of chancery over infants. We reconcile it with legal-historical dogmas on this basis. But the jurisdiction of equity over infants was not a factor in creating it. It arose on the criminal side of the courts because of the revolt of those judges' consciences from legal rules that required trial of children over seven as criminals and sentence of children over fourteen to penalties provided for adult offenders[1].

One should compare with these the creative judicial empiricism of the praetor's edict. Some lawyer, urged by the claims of some particular client, conceives what will meet the needs of his client, argues for it and persuades a praetor. A new idea comes into the law with the remedy applied to that case. Sometimes we know who invented what became the basis of a long juristic development and wrote a chapter in the law. Thus in the *actio Serviana* a concrete remedy was invented for a case that called for more effective legal relief. It was carried forward in the *actio quasi Serviana* by an analogy bordering on fiction. Then jurists, with the picture of natural law before them, put a generalization behind it and a whole theory of pledge resulted[2]. Today the Romanist puts tacit hypothecation to as many uses as we do constructive trust[3]. But the idea did not create the *actio Serviana*. That resulted from a reaching out for a concrete remedy to satisfy a special demand. This is brought out in another way if we compare tacit hypothecation with constructive trust. Each achieves much the same results; each is used remedially to prevent unjust enrichment of one person at the expense of another. Yet note how different the two are in legal idea. According to the one way of proceeding it is conceived that A's property is subject to a real duty—a duty resting on the *res* as against the whole world—to answer for

[1] Mack, "The Juvenile Court," 23 *Harvard Law Rev.* 104 (1909); Flexner and Baldwin, *Juvenile Courts and Probation*, 1–7 (1915); Eliot, *The Juvenile Court*, 1–2 (1914).

[2] *Inst.* 4, 6, § 7. Note also the *interdictum Salvianum*, *Inst.* 4, 15, § 3, the name of which tells a like story.

[3] Windscheid, *Pandekten*, I, §§ 225–229.

a duty which in justice and equity is due from A to B. According to the other it is conceived that A has something which he is personally obligated to hold not for his own benefit but for the benefit of B. There is a fiction in each case—a fiction that something has been pledged which has not been pledged or a fiction that something is held in trust where there is no trust. Yet historical jurists saw an idea in each case which fixed the lines of legal development.

Jhering called creative juristic science by the suggestive name of juristic chemistry[1]. That is, it is a combining of chosen elements of the law, as it were, to make new compounds. But it often goes further and brings in elements from without and develops them by analogy or combines them with elements at hand in the law to make even more novel compounds. Instead of these compounds resulting from the unfolding of an idea, they are oftenest the result of endeavour to provide for a concrete case, leading to the application of a concrete solution, behind which others proceed to put tentative generalizations until finally the more inclusive order is worked out. Thus when we look back at it we say that an idea was realizing. But the idea served after the event to order and arrange and make intelligible. It had no part in the creation which was the act of a man seeking to satisfy a demand.

American law has notable examples of the creative possibilities of two other forms of juristic activity. At a time when it was a serious question whether American states would receive the common law of England in view of political bitternesses, hostility to things English after the Revolution, and the aversion to technical learning and special professional competence that was so marked in the Jefferson Brick era of American politics, Joseph Story, by a creative use of comparative law, was able so to expound English commercial law and English equity as to make them appear a body of universal principles, sanctioned by experience and received by the reason of mankind, and to make straight the way for their reception[2]. Here also it might

---

[1] *Geist des römischen Rechts*, III, 2nd ed. 11 (1871).
[2] See Pound, "The Place of Judge Story in the Making of American Law," 48 *American Law Rev.* 646 (1914).

be said that the comparative law invoked was something of a fiction, analogous to natural law. An ideal of what the law should be, drawn from examination of the English law in the light of the commercial law of continental Europe and of English equity in the light of the treatises of the civilians, was used to give shape to English doctrines and rules with reference to American wants so as to make them worthy of reception. Recently another form has become effective in studies of particular problems published in legal periodicals. What may almost be called the classical example is the paper on the Right of Privacy in which Mr Justice Brandeis, then at the bar, was a collaborator. A bit of juristic reasoning on the analogy of the legal rights that secure other interests of personality, showing that there was an interest in or claim to privacy as a part of personality and postulating a legal order that secures personality completely, created first discussion, then a conflict of decision, and finally through judicial decision or statute a new chapter in the law of torts[1]. A similar case is to be seen in Judge Smith's paper on negligent use of language, which has already found judicial following[2]. Examples might be multiplied.

Creative legislation is a phrase of more familiar sound. The constitutional dogma of separation of powers makes the orthodox Anglo-American lawyer loth to concede that law may be made by any one or by anything but the legislature, and the dogmatic fiction of pre-existence of the rule when a court has formulated it and applied it in the decision of a cause, makes it the harder to think of something which, however real in fact, is in inconvenient contradiction of legal theory. The proposition that legislation may create law encounters no such difficulties. Yet legislation is perhaps the least creative of the three. Indeed the historical school denied it any creative rôle and held that it could achieve nothing more than to give better form to the results of judicial and juristic development and carry out the

[1] Warren and Brandeis, "The Right to Privacy," 4 *Harvard Law Rev.* 193 (1890), adopted in *Pavesich v. New England Ins. Co.*, 122 *Georgia Reports*, 190; *Foster Milburn Co. v. Chinn*, 134 *Kentucky Reports*, 424; *Munden v. Harris*, 153 *Missouri Appeal Reports*, 632. See also the statute of New York, *Binns v. Vitagraph Co.*, 290 *New York Reports*, 51.

[2] "Liability for Negligent Language," 14 *Harvard Law Rev.* 18 (1900), followed in *Cunningham v. Pease*, 74 *New Hampshire Reports*, 435.

logical implications of ideas that had unfolded in experience and had been formulated in judicial decision or juristic writing. This theory was not unnatural in those who had been trained in Justinian's legislation, which was of this type. But there are two types of legislation, an organizing type, such as the historical school conceived, and a creative type. If one doubts the existence of the latter, it is enough to refer him to the Workmen's Compensation Acts. The principle of that legislation is now urging for other cases such, for example, as accidents in the operation of transportation enterprizes as public utilities. It has become settled in the law. But these statutes are not an organizing of the applications of a traditional idea. They introduce a new idea, or rather a new liability behind which we must put an idea to make it intelligible and to find a place for it in the legal system. Judge Smith proposed that we limit the name Torts to cases of culpable causation and set up a new category for liabilities without regard to fault[1]. Thus we should find a common idea in responsibility for the torts of servants, in workmen's compensation, in the doctrine of *Rylands* v. *Fletcher*, and in liability for trespass of animals. Yet orthodox Anglo-American theory treats the first of these from a wholly different standpoint, assimilating it to liability created by exercise of a power of representation conferred on an agent. Mr Justice Holmes[2] and later Dr Baty[3] have exposed the dogmatic fiction on which this treatment rests. The fact, however, that the law does so explain this form of liability without fault, is enough to show that no analogy and no idea of such a category was before those who devised workmen's compensation as a practical solution of a concrete problem.

To look at the subject in another way we may see the personal stamp of the great lawyer upon every legal system. The personality of Labeo, of Julian, and perhaps of Papinian has entered into the Roman law. The stamp of Tribonian is on the Corpus Juris and thus on the great quarry of legal materials for the modern world. The stamp of Du Moulin and of Pothier

[1] "Tort and Absolute Liability," 30 *Harvard Law Rev.* 241, 319, 409 (1917).
[2] "Agency," 5 *Harvard Law Rev.* 1 (1891); *Collected Papers*, 81.
[3] *Vicarious Liability* (1916).

is on French law. To mention no others, Henry II and Coke
and Mansfield stand out as personally responsible for things
of the first moment in English law. In American law Marshall
has been pronounced rightly the creator of the constitution in
the sense that his statesmanlike legal exposition of it in the
formative period made it an effective instrument that stood the
test of civil war. Kent and Story were the chief actors in the
reception of English law in the fore part of the nineteenth
century, without whom it might not have been complete.
Shaw and Gibson and Ruffin and later Doe left their mark upon
the law of their jurisdictions and to some extent upon the law
of the whole country. Indeed Doe's achievements in procedure
are a striking testimony to what a masterful personality, joined
with sound legal instincts and thorough knowledge of the
traditional legal materials, may do in the way of practical law
reform by judicial decision alone, without the aid of legislation.

But Henry II and Coke will best make the point. Granting
that centralization in England was inevitable for any reason that
you will, three types of centralization were possible. There
might have been a judicial legal centralization with decentralized
administration, as in England, or administrative centralization
with decentralized justice, as in France of the old regime, or
a complete centralization as in France of today. Norman
centralization in England was at first administrative. That
centralization in England became legal and judicial, a centralized
justice and one law with local administrative autonomy, must
be attributed to the masterful king, by instinct a lawyer, who
turned the English polity in the direction of legal unification
at the critical moment. Coke's personal achievement is even
more clear. His vigorous personality, his minute knowledge
of the legal materials, the ascendancy which his professional
standing gave him, and his power and determination to wield
it to make a judicially administered law of England in which
courts should stand between the individual subject and the
crown and the crown's agents, by interpretation and logical
development of medieval English materials, actually made law
as perhaps it was never made to so great an extent by one man
before or since. When modern writers show how little basis

there often is for Coke's assertions in the authorities he cites or expounds, they testify to his creative power. For Coke's version superseded the medieval authorities as a statement of the law. Hobbes says that authority not truth makes the law[1]. A clear vision of the demands to be met, a clear conception of how to meet them and a mastery of the legal materials, making it possible to select them with assurance and combine them with confidence, may make law in despite of both authority and historical truth. That Coke could do this in the face of determined opposition is a clear proof of the efficacy of creative effort by a strong man.

Yet it would be possible to make extravagant claims for such an interpretation, as for each of those heretofore considered. I would not urge the great-lawyer interpretation for a moment as the one explanation of legal phenomena, the one method of writing legal history. What I do urge is the importance of looking at the events of legal history in terms of the men who took part in them and of the personalities and characters and prejudices of these men as a factor in the results. For we need to bear in mind what Coke and Mansfield were able to do, the one to give an authoritative form to the legal results of the strict law, the other to liberalize the law so formulated and make it a law that could go round the world in the nineteenth century. The legal achievements of the nineteenth century must be organized and restated presently to serve as the basis for another judicial and juristic new start. The law must be liberalized once more and must receive new and large infusions from without, after a century of pruning away archaisms and of organizing and systematizing rather than creative juristic activity. These demands of the immediate future will call for men and for a faith in the power of men to do great things which was wanting in the legal science of the last century.

[1] *De Cive*, cap. XIV, § 1.

VII

AN ENGINEERING INTERPRETATION

IF the argument up to this point has been sound, we require an interpretation of legal history that will take account of the men who act in finding and adapting legal materials, of the materials with which they act, of the circumstances under which they act, and of the purposes for which they act. Many of these requirements are met by Kohler's civilization interpretation, which was urging by the Neo-Hegelian wing of the social-philosophical jurists and attracting many adherents in the first decade of the present century. Hence we must examine and appraise that interpretation before suggesting a new one.

Kohler was exceptionally qualified as a philosopher of law in respect of all-round knowledge of legal materials and acquaintance with the problems of the legal order. He was first an *Amtsrichter* or, as we might say, county-court judge. Then for five years he was *Kreisrichter* or superior judge. He became professor at Würzburg in 1878 and at Berlin in 1888, where he continued till his death in 1919. He worked first in Roman law, then in primitive law, in which he became one of the first authorities[1], then in specialized branches of the law, such as the history of criminal law[2], patent law on which he wrote a well-known treatise[3], and bankruptcy on which also he wrote a standard text[4]. Later he taught the new German code of 1900 and wrote a commentary thereon[5]. Finally (1904) he

---

[1] *Shakespeare vor dem Forum der Jurisprudenz*, 1883, 2nd ed. 1919; *Rechtsvergleichende Studien über islamitisches Recht, das Recht der Berbern, das chinesische Recht und das Recht auf Ceylon* (1889); *Zur Urgeschichte der Ehe* (1897); Kohler und Peiser, *Aus dem Babylonischen Rechtsleben* (1890–1898); Kohler und Ungnad, *Assyrische Rechtsurkunden* (1913).

[2] *Studien aus dem Strafrecht* (1890–1897).

[3] *Forschungen aus dem Patentrecht* (1888); *Handbuch des deutschen Patentrechts* (1900).

[4] *Lehrbuch des Konkursrechts* (1891); *Leitfaden des deutschen Konkursrechts* (1893, 2nd ed. 1903).

[5] *Lehrbuch des bürgerlichen Rechts* (1906).

began to write upon the philosophy of law[1]. He came nearer than any one else in modern times to taking all law for his province.

Brought up in the historical school, Kohler was among the leaders of those who in the latter part of the nineteenth century sought to give that school a broader basis and less rigid method. When the school began to break up, some going over to positivism, some to a Neo-Kantian social philosophy of law, and some to a revived natural law, he sought to carry forward the best of the traditions of the school by means of a Neo-Hegelian social-philosophical jurisprudence. He attacked both the metaphysical-historical natural law and the analytical comparative law of the last generation. The legal science of the nineteenth century, he said, took historical materials and materials derived from analytical investigation of existing systems of law and made from them a new natural law, that is, an assumed body of universally valid legal principles and universal legal institutions. But the seventeenth- and eighteenth-century natural law, which was to be deduced from the nature of man, did not criticize law on the basis of itself in this way. It went outside of the law for its critique. In the nineteenth-century philosophy of law, on the other hand, the law was criticized by an ideal form of itself. Hence philosophy of law in the last century was relatively barren of results whereas seventeenth- and eighteenth-century philosophy of law achieved great things. For while the latter sought to make positive law in the image of an ideal, the former made an ideal in the image of the positive law. Nor did the so-called comparative method, from which so much had been expected, prove more fruitful. As philosophy of law turned to specious justifications of what existed, comparative law gave "sham reconciliations" by comparing the content of legal precepts as abstract propositions, apart from their social history and social operation, as if all rules had come into existence at one stroke—let us say in Cloudcuckootown—and then found

[1] "Rechtsphilosophie und Universalrechtsgeschichte," in Holtzendorff, *Encyklopädie der Rechtswissenschaft*, I, 6th ed. 1907, 7th ed. 1913; *Lehrbuch der Rechtsphilosophie*, 1908, 2nd ed. 1912, transl. by Albrecht as *Philosophy of Law*, 1914.

specious reasons for them by which they might be reconciled or unified[1]. In other words there was comparative analysis and analytical comparison. Such was the comparative law of a generation ago—a very different thing from the comparative law with a philosophical, historical and sociological background for which Kohler contended and which he was so largely instrumental in bringing about.

Everyone had begun to say that law was relative. But relative to what? Kohler answers that it is relative to civilization and laws are relative to the civilization of the time and place. There is no universal body of legal institutions and legal rules for all civilizations. Instead there is a universal idea, namely, human civilization. "Different in its details," he says, law "is alike in the fundamental quest, that is, the furthering of civilization through a forcible ordering of things[2]." Hence if there is no natural law, there is still the constant factor of the relation between law and civilization, "a relation which takes on a different content with the infinite variety in the conditions of human cultivation[3]." But law is not only a means toward civilization, it is a product of civilization. We must look at it, therefore, in three ways: as to the past, as a product of civilization, as to the present as a means of maintaining civilization, as to the future as a means of furthering civilization[4]. Observe how the historical, the nineteenth-century analytical and the sociological points of view are united in this theory.

At this point one will ask, what does Kohler mean by civilization? He replies that it is the social development of human powers toward their highest possible unfolding[5]. This leads to a further question how height is to be determined in such a

[1] "The lack of vision that made men think it possible to construct a philosophy of law without philosophy took a bitter revenge. Natural law arose once more in a new form and led to a sort of positivist philosophy of law. Natural law could not be identified with positive law. But a decoction was made from different legal systems and legal postulates and was then called philosophy of law....Similarly barren are the writings of Merkel who tried to construct a universal theory of law out of a scanty knowledge of a few legal systems and by his sham reconciliations contributed to the decay of juristic thought." *Lehrbuch der Philosophie des Rechts*, 16.
[2] *Moderne Rechtsprobleme*, § 1, 1907, 2nd ed. 1913.
[3] *Ibid.*   [4] *Lehrbuch der Rechtsphilosophie*, 1–2.
[5] *Moderne Rechtsproblem?*, § 1.

connection. Apparently he means the most complete human control of nature, including human nature, for human purposes[1], and in this respect there seems a point of contact with the so-called economic realists in jurisprudence, who find the end of law in a maximum satisfaction of human wants. Also superficially there seems a connection with the doctrine of the Krauseans. Thus Lorimer says that the ultimate object of jurisprudence is the attainment of human perfection, adding that this object is identical with the object of ethics[2]. That is, the object of ethics is to perfect individual conduct by the perfection of the individual; the object of jurisprudence is individual perfection by the perfect relation between the individual and other individuals. As Ahrens saw it, the individual was perfecting himself and the law was keeping others off while he did so and that he might do so[3]. The individual was the organ of humanity and humanity was perfected as the individual perfected himself. Undoubtedly there is truth in this. One great agency in social progress is individual spontaneous initiative. Hence the social interest in individual free action as part of the interest in the individual life. But Kohler's point is that there is much more than this. We are not merely a mob of individuals each seeking to perfect himself. There is an idea of civilization at work. A whole people, a whole human race, is trying to lift itself up by developing its powers to their highest pitch. It is not merely that we keep the peace while each prosecutes his individual search for perfection, whether by social or anti-social paths. Such was the conception of the function of law that led to juristic denunciation of sanitary laws and factory acts. Rather each and all are developing the whole through many means and among these are legal institutions and political institutions which express, maintain and further, or are designed to further, civilization as it is understood by them in their time and place.

According to Kohler the task of the legal order is two-fold[4].

[1] See Berolzheimer in *Archiv für Rechts- und Wirtschaftsphilosophie*, III, 195–196.
[2] *Institutes of Law*, 2nd ed., 353, 1880.
[3] *Cours de droit naturel*, 8th ed., § 19, 1892, 1st ed. 1837.
[4] *Lehrbuch der Rechtsphilosophie*, 1.

First, it is to maintain existing values of civilization. This is what the Greeks, and the Romans and the Middle Ages following them, saw as the end of law. Second, it is to create new ones—to carry forward the development of human powers. This is analogous to Ward's idea of the efficacy of effort. It will be perceived that in place of the simple idea of freedom—of individual self-assertion—from which the metaphysical school started or which it saw realizing in legal history, we have here a complex idea of continually advancing civilization, of infinitely progressing human development of human powers. The idea is not a simple idea whose narrow bounds have been fixed once for all but a complex, growing idea. One is reminded of William James's suggestion of a growing God. If this interpretation like all idealistic interpretations substitutes a renamed god for the divine authority of the beginnings of law, at least it is a god that grows and that does not jealously deny effectiveness to human action.

It has been suggested that Kohler goes back to the conception of law in the ancient city-state, as, for instance, when he says that "human civilization is only conceivable if there is a system among men which assigns each man his post and sets him his task, and which takes care that existing values are protected and that the creation of new ones is furthered[1]." This sounds not unlike some things in Plato's Republic[2]. But there is a fundamental difference. The idea of Greek philosophers and Roman lawyers was one of an ideally stationary society which from time to time would go wrong and had to be corrected with reference to the type. As in a Hindu village-community periodical re-distribution becomes necessary because in time the partition or destruction of households has produced a situation out of accord with the design[3], so it was necessary to re-distribute society occasionally as the type was departed from—to put each man in his appointed groove, as determined by his nature, and to keep him there. This is not at all Kohler's idea. Civilization moves forward. But its progress is not a simple advance. "Its development," he says, "proceeds in such wise that the

---

[1] *Id.* para. 6.   [2] E.g. III, 397–398; IV, 434.
[3] See Mayne, *Hindu Law and Usage*, 8th ed., 300.

seeds of the new are already at hand in what exists and as one grows and the other decays new values are continually made out of the old[1]." It is not that we may have once for all an ideal society with every one in his place and the law to keep him there. Yet we cannot develop the utmost that is in human powers in a mad scramble in which values are lost by friction and waste. We must have a certain ordering of human activities that puts limits to human action, that assigns each to do things in order to protect existing values and to further the creation of new ones. How far this ordering shall go must depend on the civilization of the time and place, on the values to be conserved and the means at hand to create new ones. In rural, pioneer, agricultural America of the fore part of the last century, there was no occasion to limit the contracts a labourer could make as to taking his pay in goods. To have done so would have been arbitrary. In urban, industrial America of the twentieth century, on the other hand, a regime of abstract freedom of contract between employer and employee often led to a destruction of values. It led to sacrifice of the social interest in the human life of the individual worker. Hence it was not unreasonable to put limits upon what employer and employee might contract. Moreover, Kohler does not say that the law is to assign each man his post and set him his task. But there must be some system that does this. It may be done by political or politico-military machinery, as in the extreme case of Sparta; by tradition and stratified society resting on authority, as in the Middle Ages; by free competition, as we sought to do in the nineteenth century, or by an economic regime as today. In any event it is the place of the law to uphold that system so that civilization may be maintained and furthered. This does not exclude individual initiative to find one's place or make one's place nor does it require a social ordering through the law that puts men in predetermined places and keeps them there. We are not required to make a final and absolute election between two strictly defined alternatives. Each may be destructive of values. If the latter may cut off a main spring of social progress and repress individual self-assertion to the point of stunting the

[1] *Lehrbuch der Rechtsphilosophie*, I, para. 5.

individual life, the apotheosis of individual free initiative in the last century caused us to lose sight of the social interest in the human life of the concrete man in our zeal for the abstract freedom of the abstract man.

For example, in the chapter entitled Sanitary Supervision in Spencer's *Social Statics*, we are told in effect that it is better that the poor of our cities should die in epidemics than that state boards of health should curtail individual freedom or interfere with individual initiative or want of initiative; that it is better that small pox should ravage the community than that an individual should be made to vaccinate[1]. Legislation should not impose restrictions; it should remove those restrictions on the free action of individuals that are not needed to secure like freedom on the part of his neighbours. Despite such theories, however, the law has never been able to carry the proposition that every one is the best judge of his own happiness, and hence should contract as he chooses, beyond a certain point. Minors have no judgment. Persons under economic duress have no real freedom. As Lord Northington put it, necessitous persons are not free[2]. Irish tenants and American-Indian allottees of land, turned overnight into proprietors, had had no sufficient experience of freedom. There are other social values than a complete abstract freedom of contract. A change of attitude in legal thinking throughout the world, which marks twentieth-century jurisprudence, rests on recognition of the social interest in the individual life as something broader and more inclusive than individual self-assertion. Kohler would say that it is a question of time and place whether it maintains and furthers civilization to leave men wholly free to contract as they choose or whether the legal order should hold down their self-assertion in certain situations and for certain purposes.

Yet important as it is not to lay down dogmatically an abstract scheme of universal law, something more definite than a conception of maintaining and furthering civilization is needed for the immediate purposes of jurisprudence and legislation. The

[1] 1892 ed., 197–216 (written 1850).
[2] "Necessitous men are not, truly speaking, freemen, but, to answer a present exigency, will submit to any terms that the crafty may impose upon them." *Vernon* v. *Bethell*, 2 Eden, 110, 113 (1762).

judge must have a more detailed picture in his mind to guide him in finding legal rules, in interpreting them and in applying them to the decision of causes. The legislator must have a more detailed picture to guide him in law-making. The jurist also must have a clear picture whereby to lay out the lines of creative as well as of ordering and systematizing activity. It is well that the jurist, at least, should recognize that it is but a picture for use in the time and place and that his mind should be reasonably open with respect to the possibility of repainting it in whole or in part. Still he must have some such picture, and will be governed by one whether he is aware of it or not. Kohler, carrying out his interpretation, meets this need with his theory of the jural postulates of civilization. The civilization of every time and place has certain jural postulates—not rules of law but ideas of right to be made effective by legal institutions and legal precepts. It is the task of the jurist to ascertain and formulate the jural postulates not of all civilization but of the civilization of the time and place—the ideas of right and justice which it presupposes—and to seek to shape the legal materials that have come down to us so that they will express or give effect to those postulates[1]. There is no eternal law. But there is an eternal goal—the development of the powers of humanity to their highest point. We must strive to make the law of the time and place a means toward that goal in the time and place, and we do this by formulating the presuppositions of civilization as we know it. Given such jural postulates, the legislator may alter old rules and make new ones to conform to them, the judges may interpret, that is, develop by analogy and apply, codes and traditional legal materials in the light of them, and jurists may organize and criticize the work of legislatures and courts thereby.

Let me illustrate. We should agree, as one jural postulate of the civilization of today, that in our society men must be able to assume that others will commit no intentional aggressions upon them. We need not go about armed as men did in the earlier Middle Ages nor avoid the sky line like the savage. We go about our several businesses with a serene assurance that we shall not be attacked. Also we should no doubt agree, as a second

[1] *Lehrbuch der Rechtsphilosophie*, 1, para. 7.

postulate, that in our society men must be able to assume that others when they act affirmatively, will do so with due care with respect to consequences that may reasonably be anticipated—"due" meaning, perhaps, what is exacted by the average good sense of the community. In a world that is increasingly full of machineries and agencies of potential danger, we assume that those who operate them will look out for what might reasonably be anticipated in the way of injurious consequences, and go about our several vocations without fear. Is there a third postulate? May we say that in civilized society men must be able to assume that others who maintain things likely to get out of hand or to escape and do damage will restrain them or keep them within their proper bounds? If so, the law may well impose liability for unintended non-negligent interference with the person or property of another through failure to restrain or prevent the escape of some dangerous agency which one maintains, and the rule of *Rylands* v. *Fletcher*, liability for trespass of animals without regard to fault, and liability at one's peril for injuries through escape of wild animals which one harbours, are juristically justified. If not, all these cases should be criticized with reference to the second postulate and the nineteenth-century view that they were historical anomalies, to be limited in their application and ultimately eliminated, should be the jurist's guide. It will be said that this formulation of the jural postulates of civilization gives us natural law once more. It does. But it is a natural law drawn from observation of the concrete civilization of the time and place and endeavour to ascertain the ideas of right which it presupposes, whereas the eighteenth-century natural law was a deduction from the nature of the abstract man. Also it is a practical natural law and, as it has been put, a natural law with a changing or a growing content[1]. The revival of natural law in the present century is not a revival of the rigid natural law of the metaphysical school in the last century and ought not to be a revival of the universal natural law of the century before. It is a revival

---

[1] Stammler, *Wirthschaft und Recht*, 2nd ed. 180–181, 1905 (1st ed. 1896). See also Saleilles, *L'École historique et droit naturel*, *Revue trimestrielle de droit civil*, 1, 96–99 (1902).

of the creative natural law of the seventeenth and eighteenth centuries, but as something relative not something that shall stand fast forever[1]. Thus the method of formulating the jural postulates of the civilization of the time and place is one of the most important achievements of recent legal science.

You will have perceived how much nearer Kohler's interpretation comes to meeting the requirements we have laid down than any which went before it. Indeed I shall not deny that I framed those requirements after comparing his with the foregoing and asking myself whether he had met what seemed defects in them and whether I was satisfied wholly with his conception. The advantages of his interpretation are clear. It recognizes the creative element in legal history, yet it avoids the confident rejection of the past and faith in rational abstract schemes, as able to stand on the basis of their intrinsic abstract reasonableness, which was the besetting fault of eighteenth-century natural law. It takes account of the need of stability through recognizing that we must work with the materials which the social and legal past have given us, and of the need of change by conceiving of law as relative to a constantly changing civilization. It does not hold legal development down to eternally fixed paths with but a narrow margin of wandering within the two walls of each path. And yet I do not feel satisfied. It is at bottom an idealistic interpretation and I prefer an instrumentalist point of view. It treats its idea as causal not instrumental. It gives us an idea operating from within and bringing about legal development in its growth and unfolding, not an instrument by which men understand legal development after the event and organize its phenomena and make them available for juristic purposes. Hence I should fear that in common with prior idealistic interpretations it would tend to keep up the rigidities of nineteenth-century jurisprudence. Also, although Kohler himself knew law in action and legal history too thoroughly to fall into such an error, I should fear that its Hegelian form would tend to obscure the element of human activity, that jurists who accepted this interpretation would expect the idea of civilization

[1] Charmont, *La renaissance du droit naturel*, 217–218 (1910); Demogue, *Les notions fondamentales du droit privé*, 22 (1911).

to unfold itself in legal institutions and rules and doctrines and would expect things to do themselves in legal development, and so would remain in the juristic stagnation if not in the juristic pessimism of the immediate past. I concede that the Hegelian cast of Kohler's interpretation is not necessary. But there it is. And I suspect that to many the sauce will appeal more than the fish. Hence I shall venture to suggest another possibility.

All interpretations go on analogies. We seek to understand one thing by comparing it with another. We construct a theory of one process by comparing it with another. The command of the house-father or the magistrate in the city-state (e.g. the praetor's *mittete ambo* or *vim fieri veto*) or of the military commander, the wisdom of the tribe taught by the old men to the youth, or the wisdom of the people taught by teacher to pupil or of the craft taught by master to apprentice, the treaty between warring households or clans or tribes fixing the bounds of their claims to possess things or do things, the deduction of the properties of a triangle from a limited number of given axioms, the development of the plant from the seed, the revolutions of the planets in orbits which may be calculated by mathematics, the origin of species by natural selection, the struggle for existence between individual organisms and between species, the individual man with his peculiar character and temperament that enter into the work of his hands, the struggle of conflicting self-interests in economic competition—all these analogies have been used to interpret law and the history of law. We require an analogy, then, and it is an advantage to have an analogy that puts things in terms of the dominant activity of the time and so is likely to give results in accord with the life of the time to which our law is to be applied. We require an analogy also which will not postulate formal and logical determinism nor positivist determinism, and yet will remind us that what we do in law is conditioned by many things. It must give us an interpretation in terms of activity, leading us to think of legal institutions not merely as things that are but as things that are made; not merely as things that have come to us, but as things that were made at some time and are made now by those who believe in them and will them—and are largely what the latter believe them and will them to be. Yet it must give us an interpretation in terms of conditioned activity, conditioned by the capacities, the characters and the prejudices of those who plan and make, by the materials with which they must work, by the circumstances in which they must work, and by the special purposes for which they work. Such an analogy seems to me to be afforded by engineering. Let us think of jurisprudence for a moment as a science of social engineering, having to do with that part of the whole field which may be achieved by the ordering of human relations through the action of politically organized society.

Engineering is thought of as a process, as an activity, not merely as a body of knowledge or as a fixed order of construction. It is a doing of things, not a serving as passive instruments through which mathematical formulas and mechanical laws realize themselves in the eternally appointed way. The engineer is judged by what he does. His work is judged by its adequacy to the purposes for which it is done, not by its conformity to some ideal form of a traditional plan. We are beginning, in contrast with the last century, to think of jurist and judge and law-maker in the same way. We are coming to study the legal order instead of debating as to the nature of law[1]. We are thinking of interests, claims, demands, not of rights; of what we have to secure or satisfy, not exclusively of the institutions by which we have sought to secure or to satisfy them, as if those institutions were ultimate things existing for themselves. We are thinking of how far we do what is before us to be done, not merely of how we do it; of how the system works, not merely of its systematic perfection. Thus more and more we have been coming to think in terms of the legal order—of the process—not in terms of the law—the body of formulated experience or system of ordering—to think of the activity of adjusting relations or harmonizing and reconciling claims and demands, not of the adjustment itself and of the harmonizing or reconciling itself as a system in which the facts of life mechanically arrange

[1] Kohler, *Einführung in die Rechtswissenschaft*, § 1, 1902; Levi, *La société et l'ordre juridique*, 1911; Levi, *Contributi ad una teoria filosofica dell' ordine giuridico*, 1914.

themselves of logical necessity. Such a change of attitude is manifest among all types of jurists in the present century. It may be illustrated by merely enumerating the six points which are urging in the juristic literature of the day: study of the actual social effects of legal institutions and legal doctrines[1], study of the means of making legal rules effective[2], sociological study in preparation for law-making[3], study of juridical method[4], a sociological legal history, and the importance of reasonable and just solutions of individual cases, where the last generation was content with the abstract justice of abstract rules[5].

Jurisprudence is said to be the science of law. But it must be more than an organizing and systematizing of a body of legal precepts. There are three things to consider, which may not be looked at wholly apart from each other and yet must not be confused by ambiguous use of the term "law." Putting them in the chronological order of their development, these are, the administration of justice, the legal order and law. The administration of justice is clearly enough a process. It is the orderly disposition of controversies by tribunals having customary or contractual or religious or political power to pronounce between the contesting parties. It is not, however, the simple mechanical process which the last century wished it to be and vainly strove to make it. In matters of property and commercial

[1] Ehrlich, *Grundlegung der Soziologie des Rechts*, chap. 21; Ehrlich, "Die Erforschung des lebenden Rechts," Schmoller's *Jahrbuch für Gesetzgebung*, xxv, 190; Page, "Ehrlich's Seminar of Living Law," *Proceedings of Fourteenth Annual Meeting of the Association of American Law Schools*, 46; Kantorowicz, *Rechtswissenschaft und Soziologie*, 7–8; Van der Eycken, *Méthode positive de l'interprétation*, 190.

[2] Parry, *The Law and the Poor*, 248–249; Smith, *Justice and the Poor*; Pound, "Law in Books and Law in Action," 44 *American Law Rev.* 12; Pound, "The Limits of Effective Legal Action," 27 *International Journal of Ethics*, 150.

[3] Tanon, *L'Évolution du droit et la conscience sociale*, 3rd ed., 196–198 (1911); Kantorowicz, *Rechtswissenschaft und Soziologie*, 9 (1911); Willcox, *The Need of Social Statistics as an Aid to the Courts*, 1913.

[4] Geny, *Méthode d'interprétation*, 2nd ed., 1, § 7, 1919 (1st ed. 1899); Wurzel, *Das juristische Denken*, especially § 30 (1904); *Les Méthodes juridiques*, Lectures by French jurists, 1911; Bozi, *Die Weltanschauung der Jurisprudenz*, 1907; *Science of Legal Method*, Modern Legal Philosophy Series, vol. 9; Wigmore, *Problems of Law*, 65–101 (1920).

[5] Hollams, *Jottings of an Old Solicitor*, 160–162; Gnaeus Flavius (Kantorowicz), *Der Kampf um die Rechtswissenschaft*, 1906; Kantorowicz, *Rechtswissenschaft und Soziologie*, 11 ff. (1911).

law, where the economic forms of the social interest in the general security—security of acquisitions and security of transactions—are controlling, mechanical application of fixed, detailed rules or of rigid deductions from fixed conceptions is a wise social engineering. Our economically organized society postulates certainty and predicability as to the incidents and consequences of industrial undertakings and commercial transactions extending over long periods. Individualization of application and standards that regard the individual circumstances of each case are out of place here. In Bergsonian phrase we are here in the proper field of intelligence, characterized by its power of "grasping the general element in a situation and relating it to past situations[1]." For the general element in its relation to past situations is the significant thing in securing interests of substance, that is, in the law of property and in commercial law. The circumstances of the particular case cannot be suffered to determine the quality of estates in land nor the negotiability of promissory notes. One fee simple is like another. Every promissory note is like every other. Mechanical application of rules as a mere repetition precludes the tendency to individualization which would threaten the security of acquisitions and the security of transactions. Yet this is by no means the whole field of the administration of justice.

Another type of controversy involves the moral quality or the reasonableness of individual conduct and of the conduct of enterprizes. Here, in spite of all attempts in the last century to reduce every part of the law to chapter and verse of straitly defined rule, to precisely limited conceptions and to logical deduction from exactly formulated principles, legal systems have developed an elaborate apparatus of individualization. Thus in Anglo-American law application is individualized by means of at least seven agencies: by the discretion of courts in applying equitable remedies; by legal standards, such as the standard of due care, the standard of fair conduct of a fiduciary, the standard of reasonable facilities to be furnished by a public utility; by the power of juries to render general verdicts; by

[1] *Creative Evolution*, 153–173. See Lindsay, *The Philosophy of Bergson*, chap. 5, especially p. 219.

the latitude of judicial application involved in finding the law in the adjudicated cases; by devices for adjusting penal treatment to the individual offender; by the informal methods of judicial administration in petty courts; and by administrative tribunals. Here, in Bergson's phrase, we are in the field of intuition. We have to do with the element that is unique in each case and calls for "that perfect mastery of a special situation in which instinct rules[1]." No two cases of negligence are alike. It is not the general features of such cases, for which mechanically applied rules would be appropriate, but the special circumstances, calling for intuitive application of a standard, that are significant. There is nothing unique in a bill of exchange. Every case of human conduct is a unique event.

Austin was a chancery barrister and thought of law in terms of the law of land, with which equity had most to do in his time. Our chief American writer on analytical jurisprudence was also our chief authority upon the law of property, and he came to doubt whether American constitutional law, where a chief problem is application of the standard of due process of law, was law at all. Thus we got a theory of law in terms of the law of property in which at least half of the field of the administration of justice was ignored and its methods devised for and adapted to this field were excluded from the domain of legal science. What men sought to some extent everywhere in the nineteenth century Americans carried to an extreme. We strove to subject negligence to a series of detailed rules, to turn the principles governing exercise of the chancellor's discretion into rules of equity jurisdiction, to formulate the precise details of the duties of public utilities, and to lay out a series of exactly determined degrees of crime with the exact penalty corresponding to each. We are now reaping the fruit of this attempt to subject conduct to machinery in a reaction which has been turning more and more of the field of judicial administration over to executive boards and commissions and for a time threatened a reign of something not unlike oriental justice[2].

[1] *Ibid.*
[2] Pound, "Executive Justice," 55 *American Law Register*, 137; Pound, "The Revival of Personal Government," *Proceedings of the New Hampshire*

So far as it thought of the legal order, as distinguished on the one hand from the administration of justice and on the other hand from law, nineteenth-century legal science thought of it as a state or condition; as a state of reconciliation or condition of harmony between potentially conflicting wills in which each was realized as fully as was compatible with the like realization of every other. But the legal order too is a process. It is a process of ordering, in part by the administration of justice, in part by administrative agencies, in part by furnishing men with guides in the form of legal precepts whereby conflicts are avoided or minimized and individuals are kept from collision by pointing out the paths which each is to pursue[1]. Judicial, administrative, legislative and juristic activity, so far as they are directed to the adjustment of relations, the compromise of overlapping claims, the securing of interests by fixing the lines within which each may be asserted securely, the discovery of devices whereby more claims or demands may be satisfied with a sacrifice of fewer—these activities collectively are the legal order. It is one side of the process of social control. It may well be thought of as a task or as a great series of tasks of social engineering; as an elimination of friction and precluding of waste, so far as possible, in the satisfaction of infinite human desires out of a relatively finite store of the material goods of existence. Law is the body of knowledge and experience with the aid of which this part of social engineering is carried on. It is more than a body of rules. It has rules and principles and conceptions and standards for conduct and for decision, but it has also doctrines and modes of professional thought and professional rules of art by which the precepts for conduct and decision are applied and developed and given effect. Like the engineer's formulas, they represent experience, scientific formulations of experience, and logical development of the

Bar Assoc. (1917), 13; Goodnow, "The Growth of Executive Discretion," *Proceedings of the American Political Science Assoc.*, ii, 29.

As to a like phenomenon in England, see *Local Government Board* v. *Arlidge* [1915] A.C. 120; [1914] i K.B. 160; Dicey, *Law and Opinion in England*, 2nd ed., xli–xliv; Dicey, *Law and Custom of the Constitution*, 8th ed., xxxvii–xlvii.

[1] Ehrlich, *Grundlegung der Soziologie des Rechts*, 352–380 (1913).

formulations; but also inventive skill in conceiving new devices and formulating their requirements by means of a developed technique.

"In seeking for a universal principle," says William James, "we inevitably are carried onward to the most inclusive principle—that the essence of good is simply to satisfy demand.... Must not," he adds, "the guiding principle for ethical philosophy (since all demands conjointly cannot be satisfied in this poor world) be simply to satisfy at all times as many demands as we can?[1]" This seems to me a statement of the problem of the legal order. The task is one of satisfying human demands, of securing interests or satisfying claims or demands with the least of friction and the least of waste, whereby the means of satisfaction may be made to go as far as possible. It would be vain to pretend that adjudication and law-making are in fact determined wholly by a scientific balancing of interests and an endeavour to reconcile them so as to secure the most with the least sacrifice. The pressure of claims or demands or desires, as well as many things that the social psychologist is teaching us to look into, will warp the actual compromises of the legal order to a greater or less extent. But we get no peace, as it were, until we secure as much as we can and the pressure of the unsecured interest or unsatisfied demand keeps us at work trying to find the more inclusive solution. We may not expect to draw any picture of the legal order to which the actual ordering of human relations will give exact effect. There will be less of the unconscious warping, however, the more clearly we picture what we are seeking to do and to what end, and the more we are aware that the legal order is a process of adjustment of overlapping claims and compromising conflicting demands or desires in the endeavour here and now to give effect to as much as we can. In other words, our social engineering will be the more effective the more clearly we recognize what we are doing and why.

We rely upon the physical and biological sciences and their applications to augment as well as to teach us how to conserve and to appropriate and use the materials whereby human wants

[1] *The Will to Believe*, 195–206.

may be satisfied. These materials are but too limited in comparison with human demands. As in the old-time American mining community the map of a mining district shows a maze of overlapping and conflicting claims, out of which no one would have realized anything if the working of the lodes and placers, the extent of claims and the conditions of retaining them had not been ordered and regulated, so life in society shows a like condition of overlapping or conflicting claims in which the goods of human existence would be lost or wasted, or at least the satisfactions derived from them would be small, if individual application of them to individual claims and demands were not ordered. Nor may the ordering in either case maintain itself unless it effectively eliminates friction and waste in the use and enjoyment of the means at hand. Where there is not enough to go round, what there is must be made to go as far as it will. Thus it is the task of the social sciences to find out how to make the process of satisfying human claims and demands continually less wasteful, to make it go on with less friction, to make it more effective in satisfying a continually greater amount of human demand. So far as these things may be done or may be furthered by the legal order, they are the field of jurisprudence. The metaphysical school was right in thinking of a reconciling or harmonizing. Its error was in conceiving the task too narrowly and too abstractly; in believing that a universal abstract reconciling would achieve what must be done by compromises and adjustments with reference to time and place.

More than anything else the theory of natural rights, and its consequence the nineteenth-century theory of legal rights, served to cover up what the legal order really was and what court and law-maker and judge really were doing. As first conceived, natural rights were qualities of the abstract man whereby it was just or right that he should have certain things or do certain things. The abstract man in a state of nature, i.e. in a state of ideal perfection, would claim only what as a reasonable moral entity he ought to have in view of his qualities and those of other like reasonable moral entities his neighbours. Hence what these qualities implied were to be his; they were secured to him by the ideal body of legal precepts called natural law and they ought to be secured to him by the actual body of legal precepts called positive law. In truth this was a philosophical reconciling of conflicting demands with reference to the abstract demands that would be made by an ideal abstract reasonable man. It pictured an adjustment of human claims and demands by universal precepts demonstrated rationally by considering the claims of the ideal man. In the nineteenth century natural rights became deductions from the fundamental idea of freedom and a juristic problem arose of deducing the exact limits of each right so that it could be carried out logically in every direction and yet there should be no conflict. For the several deductions from freedom could not conflict. Thus the matter seemed to have been reduced to one of definition. A collateral result was to work out a practical system of "legal rights" by which individual interests of personality and individual interests of substance were effectively secured. But the attempt at exact definition of legal rights broke down because the idea was not a simple one, as was supposed, but involved a number of distinct things[1], and also because the compromises and adjustments which were called for could not be derived from the simple idea of freedom. The law books of the last century are full of curious situations of logical *impasse* to which such attempts continually led.

"Right" had come to mean too much. All the juristic writing of the last century is obscured by the ambiguity of that overworked word. We called the *de facto* claim or interest, an idealization of the *de facto* claim, as we thought it ought to be asserted and ought to be recognized, the legally recognized and legally delimited claim after the law on a balance of claims or interests had come to some practical adjustment, and a bundle of legal institutions by which that recognized and delimited claim is made effective, all by the one name of right. It would have been impossible in any event to avoid jumping from one

---

[1] See Bierling, *Kritik der juristischen Grundbegriffe*, II, 49–73, 128–144 (1883); Bierling, *Juristische Prinzipienlehre*, I, § 12 (1894); Hohfeld, *Fundamental Legal Conceptions as Applied in Judicial Reasoning*, Reprint of papers published in 1913, 1917; Pound, "Legal Rights," 26 *International Journal of Ethics*, 92 (1915).

meaning to another in the course of the same argument. But few were conscious of the extent of the ambiguity, and it was a most convenient one. Hence courts and jurists were not careful to avoid changes of meaning in the course of apparently consecutive reasoning that enabled them to give to a practical compromise, arrived at by an unconscious weighing of the competing claims, the appearance of a logically exact definition of rights arrived at by deduction. With all its convenience in this respect, however, the ambiguity was a heavy burden on the legal science of the last century. More than one interest long stood unsecured because conscientious and learned judges could not make the deductions that would provide for it without apparent violation of some "right" that seemed to stand upon a higher plane.

What courts and jurists were really doing is revealed in another way by the conception of public policy. This or that exercise or this or that application of a so-called right was forbidden by "the policy of the law." Not unnaturally courts were cautious about formulating these policies, but in course of time some ten of them became fairly well known, and as we look at them in action it is easy to see that they are recognitions of social interests—of the claims or demands involved in the existence of society[1]. Civilized society postulates peace and order. It cannot go on unless each and all are secure in doing their work therein. Hence demand for or interest in the general security, which in the common law is put as a policy of public safety. Again the social interest in the security of political institutions appears as a policy of safeguarding the interests of the crown or of the state. The social interest in the security of domestic institutions appears as a policy against those things which tend to interfere with the family relation. The social interest in the general morals appears as a policy against corruption or a policy against things of immoral tendency or against certain specific transactions which are inimical to good morals. The social interest in economic progress appears as a policy favouring free trade in chattels or against novel restrictions upon property. In practice

[1] I have discussed this subject in detail in "A Theory of Social Interests," *Proceedings of the American Sociological Society*, 1921.

the courts continually weighed these and other social interests in the scale by declaring that this or that could not be enforced or that this or that result was forbidden because of public policy. But at best this was an awkward way of putting it. Certain claims stood apart with the label of superior sanctity as "rights." Certain other claims were in the air under the name of policies. It was easy to confuse the problem by saying that "rights" were sacrificing to policy and creating an impression that "policy" meant, not something on the same plane, but expediency or some low motive of which judge and jurist should be ashamed[1]. Accordingly the last century was suspicious of any invocation of public policy. Denunciations of the conception and warnings as to the danger involved in judicial resort to it became staple[2]. None the less the courts continued to develop the old policies and worked out some new ones. Coke's observation that many things have been introduced into the common law because of "convenience" and his proposition that the law will suffer a private mischief, i.e. a curtailment of individual right, rather than an "inconvenience[3]," remained profoundly true. In practice we never carried out each so-called right to its logical consequences by a process of strict reasoning. The actual method has been one of adjustment and compromise and giving effect to as much as seemed possible on as intelligent view of all the claims involved as court or law-maker or jurist was able to take with the materials before him.

[1] See, for example, the dissenting opinions in *Arizona Copper Co.* v. *Hammer* (Arizona Workmen's Compensation Cases), 250 *United States Reports*, 400, 433 (1920).
[2] E.g. the answers of the judges in *Egerton* v. *Brownlow*, 4 H.L. Cas. 1 (1853).
[3] See *Co. Lit.* 66a, 97a, 97b, 152b, 279a, 379a. "The law will sooner suffer a private mischief than a public inconvenience." Broom, *Maxims*, 7th ed., 147; *Absor* v. *French*, 2 Show. 28; *Dawes* v. *Hawkins*, 8 C.B., N.S., 848, 856, 859; *Atty. Gen.* v. *Briant*, 15 M. & W. 185. "*Multa in jure communi contra rationem disputandi pro communi utilitate introducta sunt.*" *Co. Lit.* 70b. Note the reason for the "right" of going over adjoining land when the road is impassable, as stated by Lord Mansfield in *Taylor* v. *Whitehead*, 2 Doug. 749. Compare Cockburn, C.J., on "the extent to which it is necessary that private rights or public rights should be sacrificed for the larger public purposes, the general commonweal of the public at large." *Greenwich Board of Works* v. *Maudsley*, L.R. 5 Q.B. 397, 401. See also Lord Hardwicke in *Lawton* v. *Lawton*, 4 Atk. 13, 16 (1743).

Illuminating examples may be seen in the mooted questions of abusive exercise of rights, of recovery for subjectively manifested injuries, of invasions of privacy, and of "interest" as a justification in trade-dispute and secondary boycott cases, in which the claim of one to free exercise of his powers, even though involving an incidental aggression, and of the other to be free from aggression must be balanced. The solutions in fact proceed by subsuming each under social interests and endeavouring to save as much as possible of each. Less controversial examples may be found in privileged occasion in defamation, but here too difficult balances must be made at times and as a result there are grave differences of judicial opinion[1]. Other suggestive examples may be seen in the English law of maintenance[2], and in the history of conspiracy to abuse legal process and malicious prosecution—a "story of a long struggle to solve the legal puzzle of punishing the rogue who would kill and rob with the law's own weapons without at the same time terrifying the honest accuser or plaintiff[3]."

To go into detail, one example from modern English equity will suffice. Take the question in *Lumley* v. *Wagner*[4]. Here, on the one hand is the social interest in the security of transactions, calling on us to enforce the agreement, to compel performance of the promise that has become part of the promisee's substance, not only in order to secure the latter's individual interest of substance but to give effect to the social demand for the upholding of promises in an economically organized society resting on credit in which so much of wealth is in that form. On the other hand there is the social interest in the individual human life which requires us to put limits to the enforcement of promises where individual freedom of action is immediately involved. To enforce a contract of service specifically, to compel continuous service of a confining nature under the direction of the employer as to its details, may be so serious an interference

---

[1] *Coxhead* v. *Richards*, 2 C.B. 569 (1846).

[2] Winfield, *History of Conspiracy and Abuse of Legal Procedure*, 68 (1921).

[3] *Id.* 67.

[4] 1 De G. M. & G. 604 (1852).

with the individual human life and thus so serious an infringement of the individual interest of personality, as to sacrifice
more than we gain in upholding the security of transactions.
Thus the question becomes one of how we may give effect to
the most of these two important social interests, which looked
at singly call for different results. In such a case as *Lumley*
v. *Wagner*, where the injury to the promisee's substance is
serious and not to be measured except conjecturally for a money
reparation, while the performance is not a service involving
continued interference with liberty, the decisive consideration
may well be that the court can take hold of a negative covenant
and bring about performance as a matter of economic choice
without any more infringement of personality than is involved
in the economic choice between fulfilling a promise and payment of damages. Thus the security of transactions and the
individual life are each secured, or if the latter is somewhat
infringed, it is not interfered with sufficiently to impair the
interest as a whole on a balance of all the interests involved.
Stripped of its apparatus of authority and of technical equity
doctrine, the foregoing is substantially what Lord St Leonards
actually said. The vice of ignoring in theory what we do and
must do in the actual process of making, finding and applying
the law is shown in the deadlock between employers and employees in America and the impotence of the courts, thus far,
to provide a legal way out on the basis of common-law doctrines.
So long as the matter is treated in terms of rights, defined and
carried to their logical conclusions and beyond compromise
because they are rights, the pressure of unsecured claims and
unsatisfied demands will go on.

In the last century legal history was written as a record of
the unfolding of individual freedom, as a record of continually
increasing recognition and securing of individual interests,
through the pressure, as it were, of the individual will. But it
would be quite as easy to write it in terms of a continually wider
and broader recognition and securing of social interests, that
is, of the claims and demands involved in the existence of
civilized society, not the least of which is the social interest in
the individual human life. I have discussed this subject at

length elsewhere[1]. It is enough to say that the beginnings of law lend themselves much more to such an interpretation than to the orthodox interpretation of the last century. The Twelve Tables of Gortyn in their first section provide that one who is about to litigate over a slave shall not lead him home before the legal proceeding. Is this a securing of individual freedom of the one man or the other or a provision for the social interest in the general security? When the Roman praetor in the *legis actio sacramento* put his staff between the litigants and said "let go both of you," what was the claim or demand that was satisfying, if not that same social interest in the general security? In the Germanic truce or peace, which played so great a part in the building of our common law, what have we but recognitions and securings of a series of social interests—the general security in the house peace, the peace of the borough, the peace of the great highways and the limitations upon the blood feud; the security of religious institutions in the peace of festivals and the church peace, whereby the demand of society that its duties to God be duly performed was given effect; the security of political institutions by the peace of the *gemot*; perhaps the security of economic institutions by the peace of the market? These are weighed against individual self-assertion, that is, against the interest in the individual life, it may be more crudely but quite as clearly as in the more difficult and complicated social engineering of the legal order of today.

That an engineering interpretation might be put to ill use I shall not deny. But for a season the dangers are in another direction. We shall not outgrow the juristic pessimism of the immediate past easily nor quickly, and lawyers, who must study the past and will study it largely as the last generation interpreted it, are not likely to be over-rash in outgrowing distrust of their power to do things. Moreover, what they do must get its efficacy from courts and legislatures. More and more we must rely upon jurists for creative work in Anglo-American law. Legislatures, if otherwise qualified, can give but intermittent

[1] "A Theory of Social Interests," *Proceedings of the American Sociological Society*, 1921; *The Spirit of the Common Law*, Lecture 8 (1921); *Introduction to the Philosophy of Law*, Lecture 2 (1922).

attention to constructive law-making for the purposes of the legal order. Judges work under conditions that make it less and less possible for them to be the living oracles of the law except as they give authority to what has been formulated by writers and teachers. An interpretation that will stimulate juristic activity in common-law countries, that will bring our writers and teachers to lead courts and legislatures, not to follow them with a mere ordering and systematizing and reconciling analysis, will have done its work well. It will have done for the next generation at least no less than the nineteenth-century interpretations did for that time.

INDEX

For EU product safety concerns, contact us at Calle de José Abascal, 56–1°,
28003 Madrid, Spain or eugpsr@cambridge.org.

www.ingramcontent.com/pod-product-compliance
Ingram Content Group UK Ltd.
Pitfield, Milton Keynes, MK11 3LW, UK
UKHW010047140625
459647UK00012BB/1656